Unparalleled Parallels

Two Masters - One Message

This book is dedicated to my late husband
Gopalakrishnan Iyer

Unparalleled Parallels

81=18

pramila iyer

PARTRIDGE

To order additional copies of this book, contact
Partridge India
000 800 10062 62
orders.india@partridgepublishing.com

www.partridgepublishing.com/india

Contents

PREFACE

As I write this preface, I have this exhilarating feeling of finding some purpose of my existence on this earth; even if it is just miniscule. A journey of more than 40 years in spirituality is holding me in its loving embrace and showering inexplicable joy and deep contentment and gratitude to life in its myriad forms. I give the readers a quick flashback of my life, so as to understand the background about the evolution of this book.

*My early spiritual quest

My spiritual journey started when I was in school. Unknown to myself, I had set upon my inner quest. I found myself totally lost when I listened to Swami Chinmayananda giving discourse of Bhagwad Gita in Matunga, a suburb of Mumbai. I was 'lost' because I could not understand much of what he talked about and 'lost' also because his voice and oratory swept me off my feet. I now understand that more than understanding is the power of the person who speaks with great authority and authenticity.

I came to Pune in 1976 with my first son, who was hardly a year old then. My second son was born in 1977. Looking after two small children, especially very active boys had its impact on my health. I joined Vivekananda Kendra, Pune to learn yoga to get rid of my back ache. The missionary zeal with which the volunteers worked for downtrodden people touched me deeply. Eventually, I became a yoga teacher and it gave me many opportunities to work in remand home for boys and girls.

*My deep conviction

Spirituality has a beginning; does it have an end? To my understanding there is no end. It is joy and more joy and love and more love for God's creation. I now know for sure that the only proof of my love of God is my love for His creation. If I do not love His creation, my love for Him has neither any meaning nor any purpose. This is my firm conviction. This strong conviction opened new doors to doing my little bit to the less fortunate and I had many opportunities to work for the remand home for boys and girls, orphanages, animal shelter, local jail etc. I unknowingly entered a world full of seasoned criminals and innocent victims of circumstances. I knew I had entered a different world, where indifferent people lived.

I have seen babies weighing just 800 grams. It was first-hand information for me and not a news item in a daily news paper or electronic media. Like Prince Siddhartha, who later became Lord Buddha, my young mind started searching and seeking a way out of misery. This first-hand experience of seeing the plight of innocent, abandoned and unwanted children and utter callousness of people around touched the deepest part of my being, my soul.

Having a very supportive husband and two wonderful boys (who never demanded too much of my time with them) helped me to be a person who could see beyond one's own small little family. Thus 'Vasudeva kutumbakam', which means that 'the world is my family' blossomed silently in my heart. Remand Home for boys and girls took me to yet another hell on earth. I felt that here, an army is sent to catch a mosquito, while a man-eating big fat crocodile is allowed to go scot-free. I thought that simply shedding tears and harbouring sympathy are not going to help them.

I decided to bring back some cheer into these innocent lives, even if it lasted only a few hours of my interaction with them. I knew that God did not create this earth for us to suffer. Can I do something for God's creation? I knew I was born only to do my little bit to the kingdom of god. Learning Reiki and basics of homeopathy helped me to treat minor ailments or injuries of children, animals and birds.

*My further journey

During 1993-94, I went through a 21-day course called Siddha Samadhi Yoga (S.S.Y.) developed by Guruji Rishi Prabhakar. I was thrilled so much by the contents of the course that I decided to become a teacher. The main message I grasped from SSY was how to live like a 'karma yogi' while living the life of a house-holder. Eventually, I did become a teacher of SSY and that gave me one more chance to serve; this time, the inmates of Yerwada jail in Pune.

Teaching the essence of SSY to adults posed its own problems. Till then I had worked for children under 16 years of age. In the Yerwada jail, I was interacting with criminals, druggists, rapists and murderers. Unimaginable anger and hatred was lurking in every cell and fiber of the inmates. There were also innocent victims. Understandably, they were more bitter and hateful than the others.

I tasted a bit more of hell here also. If there is godliness still prevalent, well, I saw some glimpses in the very same hell I just mentioned – the jail. Working with criminals and other inmates of the Yerwada jail showed me the tender side of human emotions beyond and beneath the tough and crude outer layers. A female, an under-trial charged for murdering a small child, was fasting for another inmate who was very sick. My faith in innate human goodness which was gasping for breath, finally did find some fresh air to breathe properly.

To me, SSY was a holy combination of wisdom of Chinmaya Mission and missionary zeal of Vivekananda Kendra all rolled as one.

In the year 2003, both my sons got married and I had more time on hand to work for the society. Just 8 years ago (around 2006) I stumbled upon a book called Tao Teh Ching by Lao Tzu, translated into English by Dr. John Wu in my son's book-shelf. Unknowingly, I had hit upon a great treasure. This was followed by another treasure in my brother's house in Mumbai in the form of one more version of Lao Tzu's wisdom expressed in the inimitable style of Dr. Wayne Dyer. The title of the book was: "Change your thoughts, change your life".

*Lao Tzu and Bhagwad Gita

Whenever I read Lao Tzu's verses, I found great similarity between the messages contained in Bhagwad Gita and the wisdom of Lao Tzu. Comparing two holy books is not a virtue, for such an act is born out of our judgmental attitude of seeing something better than the other. My train, till then, was running on a single track called Bhagwad Gita. Like a child learning to walk, I faltered and fell, feeling more confused by the word 'karma yog', (desireless action) for the essence of Bhagwad Gita is 'karma yog'. That is when I found the wisdom of Lao Tzu making more sense of the essence of Bhagwad Gita. The master's message was much easier to understand and assimilate. This is my personal feeling and I am not interested in debating with anybody on this. My journey towards Almighty now had one more track running parallel.

I started reading Dr.Wayne Dyer's book 'Change your thoughts, Change your life' with all earnestness. The first 30 chapters of Lao Tzu's translation are from this book. I was inspired by his commentary on every chapter and at the same time, I wanted to present the original text from a different perspective: the Indian perspective, if I may say so. Like a photographer shooting away a beautiful scene from different angles, I too enjoyed looking into the text from many angles. My commentary is thus 'my point of view' in more than one sense.

Till chapter 30, my husband used to read the translation for me to type. It used to take few days time for me to sieve through Bhagvad Gita and find a verse running parallel to the Master Lao Tzu's verse. Many times, after selecting one verse from Bhagvad Gita, I would find some more expressing similar thought. After his passing away there was no body to read the text. I had to strain myself into reading the original text and type the same. Neither age nor health allowed that much of a strain. That is when and why I chose John Wu's book because almost all the chapters are 'one page, one chapter' where as Wayne's book had few pages devoted to explaining the verses in his own style. Flipping the pages took more time. John Wu's book has no commentary; just translation of the text from original language to English. To enrich my understanding I read 5 more translations of Tao Teh Ching. I many times felt I was reading Bhagwad Gita. I knew I had to start penning down (typing) my thoughts. And that is what I did.

Without my dear husband, my life was as though standing on one leg. If in life I can stand on one leg, why not I try writing commentary without the help of any other text, in this case, Dr. Wayne Dyer's book?

I wanted to explore deeper without the support of Dr.Wayne's book. I decided to try my own way of searching for inner meaning according to my perception. Understanding the text and writing commentary on it was some sort of spiritual excavation for me. Precious gems are deeply hidden. It takes patience and perseverance.

This is how the title 'Unparalleled Parallels' was born. In a child-like enthusiasm I wanted to put down in words whatever I understood by comparing the two incomparable texts. A baby usually takes 9 months to come out from its hiding place. This baby mine took almost 9 years to see the light of this world. Life's biggest paradox can be found in the labour room: pain and joy existing together and I experienced that while writing this book. The delivery was assisted by Maj. Gen.Kapoor, my brother Shankar Iyer and Anthony Jerard. I thank them all for standing by me in my hours of need. Last, but not least, my heart-felt thanks to Dr. Avanish Thanawala for encouraging me and guiding me in every step. Special thanks to Mr. Sanjay Lokhande for the artwork for this book. Thank you guys, from the bottom of my heart.

Now, I place my baby gently into your hands, dear readers.

Behind all the forms was the Invisible Formless Hands of God. I offer my humble prostrations to this Super Power.

FOREWORD

Tao The Ching = Gita 'Unparalleled Parallels' is a verse by verse explanation of Tao Teh Ching by Lao Tzu, as understood by an evolved spiritualist deeply rooted in Indian philosophy. The Philosophy of Tao, which originated almost 25 centuries ago in China, is accepted globally. Lao Tzu, the revered sage, advocated self-mastery through selfless service. Bhagwad Gita, the essence of Indian wisdom, recommends and guides one to perform one's duties without desires or without expectations. While Tao Te Ching reflects Taoism of Oriental Chinese origin, Bhagwad Gita is the essence of Hinduism and Indian ethos. Both the scriptures are unique excellent classics which are unparalleled. Both have been followed by people of all classes and tastes for several centuries. Both are addressing people and situations in different times and space. Yet there is a common thread running through them. What is it? Both try and lead to the same Reality or Truth or self-realization!! The author has beautifully brought out the unified practical wisdom for the readers.

At the outset, let me tell the readers that this book was not written with the intention of publishing. It evolved from the depth of the human heart and mind searching for answers to the problems faced by mankind. The answers came in the form of realisations through intense discussions, arguments and silent meditative contemplation. After thoughtfully and painstakingly documenting them, the author realised that the simple truths which came out of the churning within her mind, can be shared and could be of great help to others also. It could guide all the co-travellers on their journey of life.

This book can help you understand some basic principles and truths of life. It gives a balanced and practical approach of living during present times. It helps one to reconcile many dualities and paradoxes which we see around us. It can guide you to peace amidst external turmoil. It helps to resolve great conflicts within and between people. This book is a good way to introduce practical spirituality to new comers. It is a self-help guide for those who have no idea of the Indian or Chinese philosophy. They can gain tremendously by reading it and studying it. Those who have already read either of the two or both the classics, Tao Te Ching and Bhagwad Gita, will relish this even more. It will help them to appreciate the fact that the underlying principles are very similar. While the spiritually inclined can read this book in a few sittings, I recommend you read just one or two verses daily and give time for contemplation. For those who are inclined towards Philosophy, it is best to make your own notes and write the questions or original insights which come up. Before the end of the book, you can find some of the answers to the questions. You will also find your own wisdom blossoming. However, the remaining questions can be resolved by you only through your own contemplation and meditation. Digesting the simple truths of life requires hard work, and it has life-long benefits!!

I find that the author has taken great pains to research, understand and explain profound principles in the most easy language. She has given practical examples from daily life. She has elaborated her commentary with stories and illustrations. While Tao Te Ching has 81 verses, the Bhagwad Gita has 18 chapters. So 81 and 18 are mirror images. Numerologically, both 8 and 1 add up to make 9, which is the highest single digit number and a spiritual number. In this book, many of the verses have been explained by quoting relevant verses or lines from the Bhagwad Gita. However, not all the 81 verses of Tao Te Ching have a corresponding verse from Bhagwad Gita.

While editing the book, I was constantly remembering Guruji Rishi Prabhakar. He was my spiritual mentor. He personified the harmonious fusion of paradoxes. On one hand, he lived and taught the Art of Non-doing. Yet, he did so much for humanity, that in the end, he achieved what an army of ten thousand cannot achieve!! Yes, he lived in Tao. He was a great Karma Yogi who went far beyond the laws of karma. Ordinary souls are incapable of comprehending the ways of the Masters and Gurus. We dare not think of judging Lord Krishna, the Sadguru, the Universal Master.

I wish all the readers a great journey into self-discovery. Enjoy the fullness by being empty!!

Dr. Avanish Thanawala, Pune. December, 2015

Introduction

1) What is Taoism and Tao Te Ching? Who was Lao Tzu?

Taoism is the Oriental Philosophy, which is of Chinese origin. Taoism is contemporary to Confucianism, and it is supposed to have its origins in Buddhism. Lao Tzu is an ancient Master of Taoism, who is supposed to have written these 81 verses of Tao Teh Ching. He was a guide, mentor and philosopher to the rulers of the Chinese kingdom. It is said that the Masters of that age believed in living in Tao, rather than writing about it. When there arose some disputes or a war-like situation in the kingdom, the Master decided to move to quieter place to be in solitude. It was only on the request of a seeker that the teaching was recorded or written. In those times, it was recorded on wooden blocks in the Chinese script, which was very difficult to engrave and decipher. Yet, one amazing fact is that over the 25 centuries of time, the 81 verses have remained intact, though there are several versions and translations of it available right now. The 81 verses have continued to guide humanity. It helps mankind to relate to the nature of Reality.

The essential difference between Hinduism and Buddhism is that while Buddhism states that Change alone is permanent, Hinduism postulates that Permanence alone exists(Advaita)

2) What is Bhagwad Gita? Who were Krishna and Arjun?

Bhagwad Gita is a complete guide to humanity for achieving the aim of life. It was delivered in the form of a discourse and a discussion by the Universal teacher Shree Krishna to his disciple Arjun. It was given over the battlefield of Kurukshetra, where the armies of Kauravas and Pandavas were facing each other and war was about to begin. At this point of time, Arjun, one of the bravest warriors in the history of mankind, is lost in deep contemplation. Seeing all his cousins and teachers on the opposite enemy side, he sits frozen. He refuses to wage a war which will kill people from both the sides, who are all his relatives. At this dramatic point of time, Shree Krishna gives His wise counsel to Arjun to fulfill his duty as a warrior. Krishna, although being a capable warrior, had Himself taken the role of being Arjun's charioteer. He reveals great insights to Arjun about how to achieve the ultimate aim of life. He explains the efficacy of doing one's duty and about leaving the results of the actions. These principles are so universal, that every human being can follow them in their own life.

3) How both can be related to the lives of ordinary citizens.

Tao does not make statements, but it shows directions and guides a person to see beyond the visible. It also questions the validity of certain norms set by man, and shows man the importance of being still and aware. It guides man to be in tune with nature. It also shows the need to do the right things at the right time.

4) Is it relevant now, for managing our lives and while working in companies and as teams?

Both Tao Teh Ching and Bhagwad Gita give vital inputs to us on the art of management and leadership. There are innumerable publications on Gita in relation to management. Tao and the art of leadership by John Heider is a fine example of how Tao can help us to manage our work and life. This is as far as we are concerned in relation with others and the world.

If we see in absolute terms, we can see our inner soul, or energy, as the ruler of our world, that is, our body, mind, emotions, relations, activities, etc. At any point of time, there are people who are dependent on us, and therefore ruled by us. There are others whom we are dependent upon, and therefore they are our rulers, literally speaking.

5) What the reader has to keep in mind while reading?

While there are plenty of insights and truths available, each reader has to think, question them, accept them and apply them in tune with his inner self. The churning between the ego and the reality has to happen in order that the wisdom is realised and it becomes a personal truth. There are no short cuts here, and each seeker has to undergo the labour pains in life. When done with meditative state, the labour of love is sweet indeed.

6) Other Acknowledgements:

Verses of Tao Te Ching are quoted from Verse 1 to verse 30 from the translations quoted by Dr. Wayne Dyer in his book 'Change your thoughts, change your Life' published by Hay House Publishers. The remaining verses from 31 till the last 81ˢᵗ are from the translation by John C. H. Wu published by Shambhala (south Asia editions).

I gratefully acknowledge Swami Swarupanada, Advaita Ashrama, Kolkatta for his wonderful commentary on Shrimad Bhagvad Gita which have been used in this book. Krishnam Vande Jagatgurum (My salutations to Krishna, the world-teacher)

Pramila Iyer 14ᵗʰ January, 2016

Mahabharat

The main characters: Though there are many personalities in the epic of Mahabharat where each one played a very crucial role, let us consider only the two clans that of Drutarashtra and Pandu.

Drutarashtra; though first born, could not rule the country as he was born blind. He had 100 sons. Eldest was Duryodhana. Pandu, the younger brother of Drutarashtra ruled the kingdom because the legal heir to the throne (viz. Drutarashtra) was born blind. He had 5 sons. Yudhistira was the eldest. By some quirk of fate, all the five Pandu brothers marry Draupadi.

The sons of Drutarashtra are collectively named as 'Kauravas', and that of Pandu as 'Pandavas'.

Lord Krishna becomes the charioteer of Arjuna in the battle against Kauravas.

Bhagwad Gita is a dialogue between Lord Krishna and Arjuna in the battle field of Kurukshetra near Delhi, India.

Now, the story, in short:

According to tradition and custom prevailing in those days, the eldest son was supposed to rule the country after the death of the father. Since the first born, viz. Drutarashtra, was born blind, the kingdom was ruled by the younger son Pandu.

Pandu also died after some years of being the ruler.

Now the question arose:

Who should be the next king? Duryodhana, the first born Kaurava, or Yudhistira, the first born Pandava?

Both the parties claimed the throne.

The Kauravas felt that treachery was the best weapon to overpower the Pandavas.

The enemy's weakness could be used as the weapon ultimate...especially if presented in such a way that the evil is veiled.

The Senior Pandava, Yushishtira's weakness was his obsessive love for playing a game of dice.

The weakness was cleverly manipulated by the Kauravas to the extent of making Yudhistira stake even his own 4 brothers and devoted wife Draupadi. He lost everything in the gamble.

Thus, the Kauravas tricked Yudhistira using his weakness for playing dice to destroy the Pandava clan. The stakes were beyond ordinary betting in this game of dice. To cut the story short, Yudhistira lost everything, including his 4 brothers and dear wife as they were indiscriminately used by the senior Pandava as stakes.

Unimaginable misfortune followed.

Draupadi, who was lost in the deceitful game of dice, was now treated with utter disregard and callousness by Duryodhana. The wife of Pandavas was put to extreme humiliation of being disrobed in the presence of her five husbands and all the gurus and other royalties.

Krishna intervened and her honour was preserved.

As per their agreement, the loser had to live in exile for 14 years. As Pandavas lost everything, they had to live in exile for 14 years.

After finishing the said term of exile, they returned claiming back their kingdom. Duryodana was not willing to give even an inch of land.

For the Pandavas, there was no other way except waging a war to get back the lost kingdom. If they won, they would get back their property. If they got killed, they would have had discharged their kshatriya dharma (duty of a warrior clan).

Thus, waging a war was the only option for the Pandavas.

This is the story of the war of Kurukshetra fought between cousin brothers. This Kurukshetra war is popularly known as Mahabharat War.

The epic says that Kauravas got Krishna's army on their side and Lord Himself became the charioteer of Arjuna.

There are many twists and turns in the story and it will be out of purview of this text to go into details. This short note is just an introduction to the Song Celestial or Bhagwad Gita which is a dialogue between Arjuna and his charioteer, Shri Krishna Himself.

Arjuna is requesting Shri Krishna to position the chariot in the middle; on one side is his own army, and the army on the other side is his cousin brothers, uncles and gurus.

Arjuna, the great warrior breaks down trembling with mixed feelings of gratitude for his gurus and love for his cousins with whom they had spent their childhood. His emotions seemed to overpower the purpose for which he was there at the first place – to destroy the Kauravas and claim back their territory.

Bhagwad Gita, the greatest gift to mankind was given by the Lord in the battle field of Kurukshetra.

There are 18 chapters in Bhagwad Gita and each chapter is called 'yoga'.

'Yoga' which is understood as some form of physical exercise is nowhere to be found in this sacred book.

Nevertheless, the word 'yoga' is repeated many times in this text. The simple understanding of this word 'yoga' is 'being united' or 'yoked".

The first chapter starts with "Vishada Yoga" or "yoga of despondency"!

What could that mean?

It means, Arjuna was so united with his own misery (of having to fight the war) that he was totally drowned, (as it were) in it. He thought that there was no hope of coming out of it. He imagined all sorts of hell for himself and his family, should he wage that war against his own people. In fact, he says; "I would prefer living in hell, than to kill my people."

Such magnanimity even while facing an enemy and that too for a righteous cause!

The message is: 'even righteous wars are to be avoided' .... in other words: 'peace at any cost'.

Hindus believe that Shri Krishna had descended on this earth to protect the good and destroy the evil. The Lord was only using Arjuna as an instrument.

In fact, all of are just instruments in the Big picture!

All Glory to the Supreme Power!

1st verse

TAO AND 10,000 THINGS

The Tao that can be told
Is not the eternal Tao.
The name that can be named
Is not the eternal name.

Tao is both named and nameless.
As nameless it is the origin of all things.
As named it is mother of 10,000 things.

Ever desire less one can see the mystery;
Ever desiring one sees only the manifestations.
And the mystery itself is the doorway
to all understanding.

The Tao that can be told
Is not the eternal Tao.
The name that can be named
Is not the eternal name.

21

If god can be given a name, for example Krishna, Buddha or Jesus, there has to be some corresponding form associated with that name. This form could be a symbol, or it may resemble a human face, a book, or a structure symbolizing the faith we follow. Once our god is confined to this name and form, we tend to discount, disregard, many times disrespect, and sometimes even try to destroy other forms or symbols of worship. Thus, god labeled, as 'my god and your god' cannot be the eternal God (Tao).

Tao is both named and nameless.
As nameless it is the origin of all things.

Hindu scriptures say: *Ekoham bahushyamaha* (one becomes many)

When we call something an apple that particular form bears the name. There are millions and millions of life forms and a handful of them have names. Invisible to the eyes are the microbes and viruses. Can anybody even imagine the billions and billions of stars and galaxies? It is beyond imagination. That which cannot be even imagined, how can that be named? Even if a man knows all the manifested things, until he realizes that the source of 10,000 things is the same, the various images of Gods will trap him and he will be strapped to his place of worship. The God, who is supposed to release a man from bondage, will tighten His grip over him and the poor soul, which could have soared so high, will only have sores in body and mind. According to Hindu philosophy, every man is potentially divine or atma swaroopa, (divine principle) irrespective of his outward qualities. Like a lamp kept in a pot, this little flame of the soul is shining in every being. Our bad actions become some sort of cover and the spark is as though hidden or appears dim. What is needed to be done is to remove the bad tendencies.

Hinduism accepts both forms of worship - *Advaita* (monotheism) and *Dwaita* (theism). The majority of people worship God as though He is different from them and because of this reverence to the Supreme Being, they construct temples and perform different rituals, like doing Poojas and chanting mantras. The human emotions are strongly revealed in this form of worship, as according to Hindusim, a person is free to worship the Almighty as child, mother, father, friend or a beloved. Many religions accept God to be a father figure and the Master. When He is worshipped as our father, we become his children. When he is worshipped as a Master, we just obey His commands. Even atheists, cannot deny the way in which the universe has been functioning for millions of years.

When we see everything as God expressed:
the bloody wars will end;
mass, meaningless destruction of resources will stop;
we can no more loot people;
there will be no rapes or murders;
reverence for every life form will surface.

I am a visible entity created by my parents. They in turn are on this earth because of their parents. Animals and birds also have parents…the lineage goes on and on…..till their ultimate creator…Who created the creation? Answer, perhaps lies in the next line:

As named it is mother of 10,000 things.

The seminal fluid of a man has millions of sperms. Hypothetically speaking, one man is enough to create all the human beings. He, at the most, can create his own species only. He cannot create mountains, trees, or other forms of animals. However, the source of all is the seed-giving Father. Nature produces them and thus nature is worshipped as "Mother nature". Mother earth is as much alive as you and me. If she were dead matter, would life spring from dead things? The sea is alive...It has million living things in it. The air is alive. It carries germs/ microbes. The rocks and mountains are alive, for so many life forms are living inside them. Everything is throbbing with life. What is not alive or semi-dead is our sensitivity. Developing our sensitivity will take us nearer to the Tao, nearer to the Mother, in this case.

Ever desireless one can see the mystery;
Ever desiring one sees only the manifestations.

The message is amazingly similar to the message contained in the Bhagwad Gita. Desireless action is the action of a *Karma Yogi*. He is constantly working, yet is neither anxious about the result nor worried about how to go about the task in hand. This does not make his actions unplanned or haphazard like that of an idiot or a fool, but makes his actions cool and collected. This serene attitude makes him achieve much without getting tensed up and straining himself in the process.

If we analyze ourselves, we will realize that many times, it is not the actions, but the expected out-come of actions which is causing us anxiety and stress.

The world is target-oriented. "Achieve this much in this much time"– when such a target is given by the boss, fear is the first reaction in the body of the subordinate. Our body is programmed to decode fear as threat to life, as though it is a matter of life and death. Our whole body gets geared up by producing more adrenaline. This hormone is meant for physical action, either of attacking the enemy or running away from the enemy. If the chemical adrenaline is not used up in the form of physical activity, it acts like a poison in our system. On the contrary, if a person meditates before taking up his work or appearing for an interview or exam, he will perform better. There are different types of meditations but the purpose of most of them is to either focus or calm the mind.

Vipassana meditation, well known in India and abroad, is about observing all the sensations experienced by our body at the present moment. So, the next time when you get a headache, try observing it. In ninety-nine percent cases, it will vanish. In vipassana meditation, there is no effort like concentration. In fact, it is just the opposite – Vipassana is about seeing it as though the ache belongs to somebody. When we just observe ourselves like this, there is no resistance and we know that what we resist persists. When there is no resistance, it follows that we feel released, relieved and refreshed. Many mental and physical diseases can be easily healed by this simple technique.

Vipassana meditation was propogated by Lord Budhha. As we are all afflicted by so many mental and physical ailments, this technique comes as a panacea to all our problems.

And the mystery itself is the doorway to all understanding.

We understand things by our five senses. Modern scientists have sophisticated gadgets to see minute things which are nearby, or even the farthest of things in the sky, but fail to see "themselves." Contrary to this is the saint, for he understands himself and thus knows whatever is to be known. This is called self-mastery, or illumination or enlightenment.

Hindu scriptures contain information on everything that exists in this world. I wonder what technology or equipments was used by our ancient seers!! Our *Vedas* are like the manuals that we get when we buy any gadget.

Desireless actions lead us to the mystery (call IT Creator, if you want to give an identity). This 'mystery' reveals things much beyond our comprehension. Lao Tzu plays with paradoxes as though to 'hit the nail on the head'. For he says - the 'mystery' itself is the doorway to understanding'. Two opposite thoughts are put together, and its impact remains with us forever.

Bhagvad Gita: 9.4.All this world is pervaded by Me in My unmanifested form: all being exist in me....(only a part of this shloka is given)

2nd verse

PERPLEXING PARADOXES

Under heaven all can see beauty as beauty,
Only because there is ugliness.
All can know good as good only because there is evil

Being and non being produce each other.
The difficult is born in the easy.
Long is defined by short, the high by the low.
Before and after go along with each other......

So the sage lives openly with apparent duality.
And paradoxical unity.
The sage can act without effort.
And teach without word.

Nurturing things without possessing them,
He works, but not for rewards;
He competes, but not for results.

When the work is done it is forgotten.
That is why it lasts forever.

Under heaven all can see beauty as beauty,
Only because there is ugliness.
All can know good as good only because there is evil

Day and night, above and below, high and low are
dependent on each other. If there is no night, there will be
no day either. If there is no death, where is the question of
somebody being born? Higher the mountain, deeper is the
valley... Life is full of paradoxes. This paradox is essential
to understand our world.

Being and non being produce each other.
The difficult is born in the easy.
Long is defined by short, the high by the low.
Before and after go along with each other......

If God produced man, who produced God?
Man ! Yes ! Man produced God for he only gave him
name and form and all the rituals to appease Him, as though
He is lacking them. His own lack became a lack for the Gods.
God is a product of man's mind. Till he understands that
"all that is, is God", his God will be 'chained' or 'limited'
by flowers adorning the idols in a temple.

The difficult is born in the easy.

According to my understanding, 'easy' is a synonym for
God. There is no effort on His part for His mind-blowing

creation. Without effort He creates and becomes everything: the stars... the moon ...the water ... everything seen and unseen. This 'Easy' (Supreme Power) easily produced 'humans' but the easily produced humans have great difficulty in finding their origin - the source - as they have cut themselves into bits and pieces in the name of religion, nationality, colour etc.

Only when we transcend the paradoxes we enter the Source of everything.

The principle of all pervading Paramatma, Supreme Being which is the essence of Hinduism, surfaces here.

So the sage lives openly with apparent duality.
And paradoxical unity.
The sage can act without effort.
And teach without words

There is a beautiful story, which I read sometime back – a master came out of his meditation of many days of silence. People gathered around him in large numbers since the morning, waiting for his message. As the master did not open his mouth, the disappointed crowd started dispersing slowly. By the end of the day, there was only one disciple left. He was so over-whelmed by the silence of his master that he cried and said: "Master! Today you spoke well!" Well, such a master who speaks without words and a disciple who understands the unspoken words are rare indeed.

Nurturing things without possessing them,
He works, but not for rewards;
He competes, but not for results.

When the work is done it is forgotten that is why it lasts forever.

We are always busy looking after the welfare of our family members. No doubt, we are duty-bound to look after them. However, the trouble is, when they leave our nest, the pain can be unbearable because of our attachment. Saints also look after people in their own way by guiding them towards liberation. Nurturing or looking after creation is the quality of any saint. The difference between the saints and the rest of us lies in the way we live in this world. Enlightened masters do not compete with others but their own selves. They have no competitors, for they are fully aware that the 'other' does not exist. They know that the very same 'Consciousness' is present everywhere. For example - If consciousness is compared to the ocean, every droplet arising out of it is its manifestation- the manifestation called man, animals, insects, rivers, mountains and all the 10,000 things.

All of us have our own ways of saying 'thanks' to God for the favours granted. "You do this dear Lord, and I shall do this for you". God and His infinite mercy is brought down to the low level of a barter system. I was also no exception until I understood my folly. There are instances in our life that in spite of intense prayers things do not happen the way we want them. When my dog fell ill, there was not one door left that I did not knock at, because I loved her so dearly! Though born a Hindu, in my desperation for saving her life, I sought the help of faith healers of other religions as well, but nothing worked and we had to say good bye. That day I realized the real meaning of 'blind love' for I blindly followed whatever I was told to do for her to recover.

Pondering over this, I asked myself -

1) Is some God more powerful than the other?

2) Is He merciful when He grants my requests and merciless if they are not granted?

Incidences sometimes become instruments in opening up new wisdom and new insights. I thank my dog who is with God now, for being that instrument. Thirty years of drowning myself in the nectarine words of Lord Krishna made me understand that the pitiable condition I unknowingly placed myself was because of my attachment to her.

Lord Krishna says: *'kripana phalahethawaha'* meaning; pitiful is he who seeks rewards for his action. (BG-2.49)

Let us compare our attitude of constantly expecting from everything and everybody around us to that of great masters.

When the work is done, it is forgotten.
That is why it lasts forever.

A story: - A Zen Master and his disciple were trying to cross a stream. They saw a woman struggling to wade through the water to reach the other side of the river. She asked for help. The Zen Master just lifted her on his shoulder and dropped her on the other side of the river. His disciple was shocked by this action, for they had taken a vow of celibacy and in that, no woman had a place in their lives. When the disciple reluctantly asked the master why he had carried her (breaking the vow of celibacy) the Zen Master said "I dropped the lady at the river-bank, whereas you are still carrying her. I wanted to do my duty of helping a person in need, while you were attached to the interpretation of celibacy as not to touch women. Your mind is still attached to the woman, while I am just walking right now."

Actions done with desires are binding, whereas actions done without desires lead to freedom. Great men of wisdom may appear to act like ordinary men, but they are detached from their actions. They do not do actions to gain pleasure, and they do not hesitate to act even if it is painful for them. They are beyond pleasure and pain, and therefore very difficult to judge by ordinary minds.

To see the flip side of the situation, let us see the story of the Yogi and the scorpion. Again two people – a Yogi and his disciple were travelling through forests and had to bathe in a river. After having bath in the river, while they were coming out, a huge deadly scorpion climbed on the Master and stung him. The Master coolly lifted it and put it back in the river waters. The scorpion came again and tried to bite the Master with its powerful sting. The Master, without anger, lifted the scorpion and put it back into the water and continued to walk. This went on for quite a few times. The disciple was disturbed and shouted at the Yogi. He was about to attack the scorpion with his stick, when the Yogi asked him to let go. The disciple was puzzled and asked the Yogi the reason behind this funny behavior. The Yogi replied: The scorpion is doing his dharma (duty) of biting me, while I am doing my dharma (duty) of letting go, not harming him and saving him! This is the level of non-violence and love for all beings that true Yogis practice, and we can learn from them.

Bhagavad Gita – Verse 2.49: Work (with desire) is verily far inferior to that performed with the mind undisturbed by the thoughts of results. O Dhananjaya (Arjun), seek refuge in this evenness of mind. Wretched are they who act for results.

2.50 Endued with this evenness of mind, one frees oneself in this life alike from vice and virtue.(part translation)

2.51 The wise, possessed of this evenness of mind, abandoning the fruits of their actions, freed for ever from the fetters of birth, go to that state which is beyond all evil.

3rd verse

CONTENTMENT IS CONTAGEOUS

Putting value on status
Will create contentiousness
If you overvalue possessions,
People begin to steal
By not displaying what is desirable, you will
Cause the people's hearts to remain undisturbed.

The sage governs
by emptying minds and hearts
by weakening ambitions and strengthening bones

Practice not doing...
When action is pure and selfless,
Everything settles into its own perfect place.

Putting value on status
Will create contentiousness
If you overvalue possessions,
People begin to steal

A story: King Janaka was considered a great ruler as well as a great saint - a gyani and tyagi i.e a man of great wisdom combined with detachment. Ashtavakra, a scholarly person, somehow felt that kingship and sainthood did not go together. He had some misgivings about the title 'Maharishi' conferred on King Janaka. Taking a chance, Ashtavakra came to have spiritual discussions with the king. King Janaka agreed and offered the scholar good hospitability – a nice royal room with many servants and sumptuous food. Next day, when they were busy in an intense discussion and debate on aspects of Philosophy, suddenly, a messenger came to inform the king that fire had broken out in the palace. Ashtavakra went running to retrieve his belongings from his room, whereas King Janaka remained unaffected by the incident. This attitude of detachment of a yogi in spite of being a king was an eye opener to Ashtavakra, for he realized that he was still attached to his belongings, while King Janaka was so very detached.

A person who is not possessive about his possessions is known as 'sthithapragnya' (one who is established in self.) Possession is not about material things alone. A man can become 'possessed' about his position and power. By hook or crook, he will try to maintain them. He is thus hooked on and his thinking gets twisted or crooked, and he becomes a 'crook'. Too much (overvalue) importance is given to power and position by people in general and political leaders in particular. Rigging of ballot boxes, buying of votes, making false voters' list are indicative of 'stealing' or overvalue attached to the people who will be occupying the chairs for a few years.

**By not displaying what is desirable, you will
Cause the people's heart to remain undisturbed.-**

When we make blatant display of wealth, there is a constant fear of thieves. When arrogance of power surfaces, it simultaneously creates people who want to topple us. A person, who can balance his power and position, without being swayed, is a yogi indeed. We also come across people who like to show off their knowledge. Such people are seldom liked by others.

A true yogi does not create ripples of rivalry or a jungle of jealousy and thus he is never a cause for disturbing others and yet plays a great role in the society.

**The sage governs
by emptying minds and hearts
by weakening ambitions and strengthening bones
Practice not doing...**

"Practice not doing"... My God! I can practice doing something like singing, cooking, teaching etc. However, how to practice 'not doing'?

'Not doing' is not the same as inaction. Inaction is tamasic ...doing is rajasic...and 'not doing' doing is satvic. In the Bhagvad Gita, the Lord elaborates on the three basic types of tendencies of people. Let us understand in a nut shell. There is no water-tight compartment as we are all a mixture of many tendencies. We are only discussing the predominant tendency of people.

1) Tamasik means darkness (not very sacred./unholy)

   Action that injure or harm others either physically or emotionally (or any other way.)

2) Rajasik means result oriented.

   Actions that are performed with desire for achieving or attaining something for one self. Most of us belong to this group.

3) Satvik means just doing allotted duty with a sense of total commitment and not expecting anything in return. Only few exalted personalities are to be found in this category.

Here again, the life of a yogi is summed up. He works relentlessly for the society, yet takes no credit, nor does he boast about the achievements. Undaunted by the tasks he has to perform, he is ever cheerful and happy. Compare this state with that of a non-yogi who also performs many actions but most of the time he is tensed-up and irritable and people find it difficult to work with him.

When action is pure and selfless
   Everything settles into its own perfect place

During natural calamities like earthquakes, tsunami etc., people muster all their resources and forgetting caste, creed and nationality, serve the needy. Although it is commendable to help others during crisis, if we develop this attitude of serving our fellow men, without waiting for a calamity to strike, what a wonderful world we would be creating! The core of every human being is love. It is his heritage. In a way, may be Tao is trying to bring out this selfless love by creating calamities. Thus, "Everything settles".....differences are settled....greed is settled... selfishness is settled. When water settles down, it becomes potable, which is its primary use. When our mind settles down, the God inside each one of us shines forth.

Bhagvad Gita: verse 12.15 By whom the world is not agitated and who cannot be agitated by the world, who is freed from joy, envy, fear and anxiety – he is dear to Me.

4th verse

TAO IS ALL INCLUSIVE

The Tao is empty
But inexhaustible,
Bottomless,
The ancestor of it all.

Within it, sharp edges become smooth.
The twisted knots loosen
The sun is softened by a cloud;
The dust settles into place.

It is hidden but always present
I do not know who gave birth to it.
It seems to be the common ancestor of all, the father
of things.

**The Tao is empty
But inexhaustible,
Bottomless,
The ancestor of it all.**

That which is empty is inexhaustible...
A paradox again...!

Tao is like electricity. Can we say it is full? It is 'nothing' (not a thing/object), yet it is the only source of all the things that run on it. Thousands of gadgets run on electricity. Similarly, all the million and trillion stars and galaxies originate from this Supreme Energy. This mighty power is what we call as Almighty or God or Tao.

**Within it, sharp edges become smooth.
The twisted knots loosen
The sun is softened by a cloud;
The dust settles into place.**

Sharp edges hurt us. The master is referring to problems in life as 'sharp edges'. But when we are deeply connected to the Source or Tao, they do not trouble us - not that problems do not exist...they do exist but we remain unperturbed for we trust more in the Higher Wisdom called Paramatma(Supreme Soul) to guide and lead us, not our small little brains. This is total surrender. Thus, 'sharp edges' become smooth. Sharp edges are external factors that affect and trouble us.

As against this, are the internal disturbances, which are mind - related. 'Twisted knots' is another way of expressing problems of life created by our minds that do not allow free flow of energy. Negative thoughts like, hatred, jealousy, fear, greed etc. disturb our mind. Many people exhibit their disgust or disapproval by making grimaces. They either pout, wrinkle their noses or twist their lips. If this becomes a habit, such facial expression is difficult to remove. But a person whose is strongly connected to Tao, is slowly released from all clutches.

The blazing sun of misfortune torches us not, for we are protected by the gentle cloud that stands between the sun and us, giving shade and shelter. In the desert of life, sand storms do occur, but again the grace quells it and we come out of it without much problem.

The message is very clear. Even saints have problems …will have problems…but because of their deep understanding of creation and the Creator, they remain unaffected.

It is hidden but always present
I do not know who gave birth to it.
It seems to be the common ancestor of all, the father
of things.

To hide a thing, we must have it in the first place. We are present on this earth with million things around us. Can there be a shadow without a substance? Can we all be present without 'That' which makes us present?

"I do not know who gave birth to it" --- I bow my head in deep reverence as I write this particular sentence for there is no way to add anything to this profound statement. How can I even think of explaining it?

In Indian philosophy god is described as parampurusha or the Supreme Man, and the earth as prakruthi or Mother Nature. In Bhagavad Gita Bhagwan says : "I am the seed giving father."

Bhagavad Gita: verse 10.3 : He who knows Me, birthless and beginningless, the great Lord of worlds – he among mortals is undeluded, he is freed from all sins.

5th verse

EXISTENCE IS IMPARTIAL

Heaven and earth are impartial:
They see the 10,000 things as straw dogs.
The sage is not sentimental;
He treats all his people as straw dogs.

The sage is like heaven and earth:
To him none are especially dear,
nor is there any one he disfavours.
He gives and gives, without condition,
offering his treasures to everyone.

Between heaven and earth
is a space like a bellows:
empty and inexhaustible,
the more it is used, the more it produces.

Hold on to the centre.
Man was made to sit quietly and find
the truth within.

Heaven and earth are impartial:
They see the 10,000 things as straw dogs.
The sage is not sentimental;
He treats all his people as straw dogs.

According to Stephen Mitchell's translation of Tao Teh Ching, straw dogs were ritual objects venerated before the ceremony, but discarded later on.

A similar ritual is practiced especially in Tamil Nadu. Turmeric powder is mixed with water and a small cone shaped object, about half an inch in height, is made and is named as Pillaiyar or Ganesha, before commencing poojas and other rituals. Afterwards this little object is dissolved in water.

The sage is like heaven and earth:
To him none are especially dear,
nor is there any one he disfavours.
He gives and gives, without condition,
offering his treasures to everyone.

The saint gives proper respect to everything that touches his life, yet, they never touch him. He possess them but he is not possessed by them.

Heaven and earth are impartial. The Sun (belonging to heaven) shines on the saint as well as the sinner. Similarly, earth also feeds both of them. Thus, heaven and earth have no favourites at all. A true saint is also impartial like them. He will serve everybody without distinction of caste and creed. Thus, he becomes universal. He belongs to all, like the Sun and the Earth.

Between heaven and earth
Is a space like a billows:
Empty and inexhaustible,
The more it is used, the more it produces.

The Master, I feel, is referring to the divine energy whirling and swirling in great waves. Hindu mythology says that the Lord Narayana reposes on a Milky ocean. If we listen keenly to the sound produced by any ocean, we will hear the sound 'uummm" or "om" which is a sacred sound to Hindus.

There are only three ways to make sound. Open your mouth and make sound...half close/half open your mouth and make sound...lastly, close your mouth and make sound... invariably we will get the sound AAA....UUU...MMM that is AUM. Aum is also written in English as Om.

We can use things which have some form. But how to use 'formless'?

Meditation is suggested by the master, for he says,

"Man was made to sit quietly and find the truth
within.

Rituals, as the master explained before, have to be discarded. It is to be used as a ladder to reach the desired place. After that, it has no purpose.

"Holding on to the centre"

A saint-poet said: "While grinding grain, the grains that are close to the centre are saved...those that are away from the centre are crushed".

Let us try to get closer to the Centre.

Bhagvad Gita: 9.29

I am the same to all beings: to Me there is none hateful or dear. But those who worship Me with devotion, are in Me, and I too am in them.

6th Verse

ENERGY IS INEXHAUSTIBLE

The spirit that never dies
is called the mysterious feminine.
Although she becomes the whole universe,
her immaculate purity is never lost.
Although she assumes countless forms,
her true identity remains intact.

The gateway to the mysterious female
is called the root of creation.

Listen to her voice,
hear it echo through creation.
Without fail, she reveals her presence.
Without fail, she brings us to our own perfection.
Although it is invisible, it endures;
it will never end.

**The spirit that never dies
is called the mysterious feminine.
Although she becomes the whole universe,
her immaculate purity is never lost.
Although she assumes countless forms,
her true identity remains intact.**

**The gateway to the mysterious female
is called the root of creation.**

This immaculate energy or Tao creates endless life forms through eternity. Gold loses its purity if it has to be made into a chain or bangle. Copper has to be added for malleability. For making clay pot, you need to add water, which means it is not 100% clay. All the things we use or consume, has its original stuff, plus something. Even if we eat fruits, our saliva is mixed with it. Thus, its purity is lost. However, this creative energy, in spite of creating millions of things for millions of years, remains the same. It is eternally 'Virgin', for it is unaffected by anything. If we can take time to wonder about this mighty force, new doors of wisdom will dawn on us.

**Listen to her voice,
hear it echo through creation.
Without fail, she reveals her presence.
Without fail, she brings us to our own perfection.
Although it is invisible, it endures;
it will never end.**

"Her Voice"....Earth is always referred here as 'mother earth' and Lao Tzu is asking us to listen to her - that means, be in nature or being with nature. When we are with it, as a part of it and not apart, we learn to respect, revere, and make judicious use of the resources available to us.

All the living beings have their own voices (or sounds) to communicate. When air blows, we call it 'wind' and it makes a whistling sound. When the wind blows, the rustling of the trees is its speech. ...every ebb and tide of the ocean, is lullaby to the restless soul. The gurgling of the rivers is the giggling sound of a teenager - so full of joy and delight! If sensitivity increases, everything (nature with all the 10,000 things) gives messages.

'The Mother' from Sri Aurobindo Ashram of Pondicherry (South India) could communicate with trees and flowers, and has compiled a book on their therapeutic values. Dr. Edward Bach, the pioneer of Bach Flower remedies has given the world 39 remedies based on different flowers. The beauty of this treatment is, only the aura or vibration of the flowers is used for healing.

Apart from nature, let us also learn to listen to people with attention and respect. The main job of a counselor is to listen to people and their version of their stories. Surprisingly, many people feel better when somebody pays attention to their woes.

Creative energy, according to kundalini yoga, lies dormant in every human being. This energy, which is supposed to be lying coiled and dormant at the base of our spine, is to be awakened only under the guidance of a master, who is adept in dealing with it. On a very gross level, it is expressed in nature as the sexual energy. Every form of art is an expression of the kundalini energy. If one becomes more creative, one helps oneself to uncoil or activate this basic power of kundalini.

Every living being creates its species. But human beings have more potential than the rest of the species for this creative energy emerges as our ability not only to procreate, but have great wisdom and develop numerous talents like singing, painting, dancing, writing, acting, imagination, visualization and much more. All of us are blessed with unique talents. This self-exploration and expression opens many pathways to the Creator, for, in one sense, we become co-creator. Unleash your potential by meditating on nature.

Bhagavad Gita: verse 14.4: Whatever forms are produced, O son of Kunti (Arjuna), in all the wombs the great prakruthi (nature) is their womb, and I the seed-giving Father.

7th Verse

INVISIBLE LIVING

Heaven is eternal – the earth endures.
Why do heaven and earth last forever?
They do not live for themselves only.
This is the secret of durability.

For this reason the sage puts himself last
and so ends up ahead.
He stays a witness to life,
so he endures.

Serve the needs of others
And all your own needs will be fulfilled.
Through selfless action, fulfillment is attained.

Heaven is eternal – the earth endures.
Why do heaven and earth last forever?
They do not live for themselves only.
This is the secret of durability.

The Tao, the Source of 10,000 things, is inexhaustible. People, animals, and all the million forms have inhabited the earth for all the millions of years. History of the world is only a few thousand years old. These few thousand years is just a small speck considering the age of our earth, and the age of the Universe or Creation.

It is very unfortunate that more and more weapons of mass destruction are created. People want to build palaces on the graves of others. Underground experiments are conducted forgetting that over the ground we live. The orphaned child, the limbless man, hungry and incapacitated old people, the terror on the faces of women …is it worthwhile? This invisible Tao becomes visible through His creation and I bow my head in reverence to all the 10,000 things. "Esha vasyam idam sarvam" is the saying from the Upanishads. It means God permeates everything. If this principle is understood at the soul level, heaven's doors open automatically.

Vidya and Vivekam are the two beautiful words about which let us get more clarity. Vidya means knowledge…not about technology or scientific advancements alone… vidya (knowledge) is: 'cobra is poisonous'. Vivekam (discriminative knowledge) is not to handle it unless I am trained to do so. Though, theoretically we know (vidya) everything is permeated by God, let us develop our discriminative knowledge (vivekam) as well. Many times, there are people who enter our lives hiding the poison in their bosom. A man of wisdom knows how to handle and move ahead, for he is immersed in Tao or the Supreme Power.

Swami Vivekananda says: "He alone lives who lives for others… the rest are more dead than alive". All the saints in every religion preached love, and are remembered hundreds of years after they left the earth because of the goodness they bore in their bosom!

Man gets and forgets
God gives and forgives

Everybody remembers God mostly to fulfill his or her desires. If we learn to be in constant touch with Him, our lives would truly be blessed.

A Sanskrit verse says: Yad bhavam, tad bhavati…we are what we think …

Mind is an extremely powerful tool that all of us are endowed with. Only 10 to 15 % of our potential is used. This massive untapped energy of more than 85 % is lying in waste. The 10 or 15% that we use is some times a 'misuse' for negative thoughts has a tight grip over us.

When even wild animals roaming in forests can be trained and tamed, can we not tame our own mind? All of us can unleash our potential and to wake up the untapped potential within us. Meditation is one of the best methods to awaken this power. For this awakening, we need practice, patience and perseverance.

This is the secret of man evolving as God.

Many religions have 'forgiveness day' (time for healing) once a year. However, if we can put it into practice on a daily basis, we can move closer to Tao!

This is another secret of man becoming God.

"Mana eva karanam manushyanam bandha mokshayoho"…says a Sanskrit verse.; meaning, mind is the only cause for binding us or releasing us. To lock or unlock a padlock, the same key is used. Which way we want to use it, is our choice.

Example: The mother is worried about her son not coming home as per his usual time. She becomes restless... her blood pressure goes up... she is always having fear about the safety of her children. She is unaware that the son is enjoying with his friends and playing cricket on the road. Every day, we have many similar experiences. Baseless fears are very deep and may need lot of counseling or other medical help to come out of this. Nevertheless, before going to others for help, if we sit and analyze ourselves objectively, we can find solutions. But our mind is weak. We need props to lean on...well...why not find your own way and live in peace.

Try this experiment: Visit an orphanage or old-age home and spend some time with them talking and inter-acting. They are there for variety of reasons. It may not be comfortable for many to share their personal problems which is the reason why they are there. Asking too many questions about their lives is also to be avoided. They also have talents. Give them a chance to share that with others. That gentle smile from otherwise unhappy face will make you feel that all the trouble you take is not in vain. And that is your gain!

Even if it is not very comfortable initially, you will be surprised how you start looking forward to being with them and the best reward is they also wait for you! Amongst all 'donations', donation of time and attention is the best. You are giving something priceless, which will never come back to you. If you spend 3 hrs, those three hours from your life is gone forever. But, Tao has different plan for such people, for everything comes back. The time donated comes back to you as a life extended, although mathematically, nobody can prove it. If this message touches your heart, start doing 'time donation'.

**For this reason the sage puts himself last
And so ends up ahead.
He stays a witness to life,
So he endures.**

Jesus says: "He who stands last, stands first"

Selflessness and sacrifice are the main qualities of a parent...especially the mothers. Even if they are very poor, they first feed the children, even if it means that they have to go hungry. Matru devo bhava, pitru devo bhava (mother is god, father is god) says a Sanskrit verse, giving first place to mother.

Indian philosophy says "Vasudeva kutumbakam" (whole world is one family). A true saint thus is like a mother, giving and forgiving. He assumes the role of a parent, and constantly works for the welfare of the people.

The whole world bows down to Mother Teresa for her selflessness and supreme sacrifice. There may be many such people doing their best for the less fortunate people. I salute them all.

**Serve the needs of others
And all your own needs will be fulfilled
Through selfless action, fulfillment is attained**

The main difference between humans and other living beings is only we can look after other forms of lives. Animals and birds can look after their young ones only. But, human beings can do service to others. Service is not about serving your own community or country, though they also deserve merit. Only when you include all forms of living and non-living, you are truly spiritual. Start with the community you live in and slowly proceed towards spiritualism, which is as vast as the sky itself.

How to serve non-living things, for example a mountain or a desert or a river? Becoming aware of their destruction or misuse by man is the first step. When the first step is taken, leave it to Tao to bring similar minded people to help you in your project. Then take the next step. If you are reluctant to take that step for any reason, join organizations that extend their hands to protect our mother earth.

There is something called critical mass i.e., when hundreds have been motivated for a particular issue – blessed are we, for we are living in the computer age where we have access to the whole world at the press of a button – this collective energy works like magic. Such mass energy can also be used for destructive purposes. Thoughts are very powerful tools in our hands. Let us use our thoughts also wisely.

Bhagavad Gita: verse 3.22 : I have, O son of Prtha (Arjuna), no duty, nothing that I have not gained; and nothing that I have to gain, in the three worlds; yet, I continue in action.

8th Verse

ALL ROUND DEVELOPMENT

The supreme good is like water,
which nourishes all things without trying to.
It flows to low places loathed by all men.
Therefore it is like Tao.

Live in accordance with the nature of things.
In dwelling, be close to the land.

One who lives in accordance with nature
does not go against the way of things.
He moves in harmony with the present moment,
always knowing the truth of just what to do.

The supreme good is like water,
which nourishes all things without trying to.
It flows to low places loathed by all men.
Therefore it is like Tao.

The earth is 75% water and so are we. Water goes to the lowest of places. From its origins high in a mountain, it runs long distances to merge into the sea which is at the lowest level and during this long journey it nourishes thousands of lives and organisms and vegetation. They say Egypt is a gift of Nile. Early settlements were always closer to water sources. In India, many worship rivers like Ganga, Yamuna etc. and are lovingly addressed as maiya or mother. It is also a tradition to offer obeisance by offering flowers etc. Water has no likes or dislikes. It offers itself totally to everybody.

Bhagavad Gita: a part of verse 7.8: **I am the sapidity in water.**

Great men are like water. They go to help people belonging to the 'lower region'. (economically backward or people who are looked down upon by the society). We have saints working for these children of God and hence, the saints are also like river, reaching out to the people in lower strata of life.

> **Live in accordance with the nature of things.**
> **In dwelling, be close to the land.**
> **In meditation, go deep in the heart.**
> **In dealing with others, be gentle and kind.**
> **Stand by your word.**
> **Govern with equity.**
> **Be timely in choosing the right moment.**
>
> **One who lives in accordance with nature**
> **does not go against the way of things.**
> **He moves in harmony with the present moment,**
> **always knowing the truth of just what to do.**

It is natural for fire to burn. It is natural for ice to be cold. Imagine if they thought of changing their nature! Ice will burn us and fire will not cook our food! Paro dharmaha bhaya vahaha says Lord Krishna in Bhagavad Gita, which means it is dangerous to follow that which is not our true nature. If a doctor wishes to construct a bridge or the engineer tries to perform some operation, they go against their dharma (dharma should not be understood as religion, though that meaning also holds good in some places...here the meaning is 'nature' or tendency; In these cases of doctors and engineers referred to above, it is their knowledge and skill in their respective field which can also be included in 'dharma'.

A doctor's dharma (sacred duty) is to heal people. If he uses his expertise in a negative way, (killing people using his knowledge) it is not "living in accordance with the nature of things"

In dwelling be close to land

Lao-tzu, the peerless Master who gave the world Tao Teh Ching, is indirectly telling us the advantages of living close to the land. Living on mountain is quite tough for many reasons. Cultivation of land becomes quite limited or difficult. Old and sick people face difficulty in climbing up and down. In case of natural calamities it will be difficult for the rescue team to reach them for aid. Building houses pose many problems. Living on mountains isolates them and trade and commerce will also face a setback. Hence, the master suggests choosing our homes wisely.

Meditating more on this sentence, I got some more insights.

May be the master is telling us to ground ourselves properly (close to the land) instead of having some impractical ideas which may not be of much use. Here, common sense is given equal importance. Being 'down to earth' is always a better option that just day-dreaming.

"Be close to the land" also points out that we should love the place where we live, as the word 'close' means closeness or love. When you love something, you look after it in a better way.

In meditation, go deep in the heart

"going deep in meditation" happens only after constant practice. What a way to suggest that we meditate regularly!

In dealing with others be gentle and kind

Connect this sentence with the previous one. Those who meditate regularly are able to go beyond the mind, which is the root cause of problems of the world. Beyond mind, there is no ego. This egolessness is the way to Tao. Sooner or later, he experiences the oneness behind the multitudes of life forms. The containers may be differently coloured, but the content is the One...the One without a second. This knowledge changes his outlook towards life itself and he sings "isha vasyam idam sarvam" (only God exists in everything) This is true freedom or liberation. Sun is mirrored in lakes, rivers and oceans and even in dirty pool water.

The wisdom that whatever he does, he does it to himself, dawns on him. He understands that for all good and bad tidings of his life, he is the author. It is he who is going to enjoy or suffer the fruits of his action.

Jesus says "forgive them Lord, for they know not what they do". When people were crucifying Jesus, did they not know that they were torturing him? They knew it very well. What they did not know, is the boomerang effect of that action, for it would certainly come back to them. Jesus in his extreme mercy, even under such excruciating pain, pleaded to the almighty to forgive them. Let us awaken this Jesus in us and bring glory to His name!

Stand by your word

Living in truth is the highest form of virtue. Islam says "A nal haque"…God is truth. Patanjali Mahamuni says "satya prathishtayam kriya phala ashritam" One who always speaks truth, he has the power of manifestation. All saints and seers live by truth. When we seek blessings from them, many of the misfortunes that we have created for ourselves not knowing the principle of oneness, are diluted if not totally destroyed. Satsang (associating with spiritual people) with great masters have this power. May we always seek the company of holy people.

Adi Shankaracharya, in his most famous verse of Bhaja Govindam says:

Satsangatve nissangatvam
Nissangatve nirmohatvam
Nirmohatve nischala tatvam
Nischala tatve jeevan mukthihi

Meaning;

Through the company of the good, there arises
non-attachment;
  Non-attachment leads to freedom from delusion
  Freedom from delusion leads to immutable reality
  Experiencing immutable reality is liberation of the soul

After a person dies, his relatives pray for the soul to rest
in peace. Living like a karma yogi will give us much more
peace while alive, than that enjoyed by the dead people,
for, we are not dependent on somebody's prayers. It is our
own effort to realize our true Self and thus we become true
masters. This mastership is attained by being a servant of
all and that is the paradox!

Govern with equity

Lord Krishna says in Bhagavad Gita: a part of verse
2.48; Samatvam yoga uchhyate) balance is yoga..
  Governing indicates position and power.
  Most of the people in power and position become
arrogant and insensitive of people's suffering. Their only
desire seems to amass wealth while still in power. Not just
politicians, but we can extend this thought to other areas
of our life as well. In factories and offices, people at the
top seldom have any cordial relation with their down-line.
They build false aura around themselves and this alienation
isolates them. In their whims and fancies, they favour people
whom they choose, even if they are criminals and anti-social

elements. Sincere workers when deprived of their dues, in due course will lose interest and enthusiasm.

Be timely in choosing the right moment

'Timely' means being always alert. Many of our regrets in life are about not doing things on time. In simple words 'we missed the bus'.

Children who do not look after their aged or sick parents when alive, feel much remorse when they pass away from this world. This deep guilt and hurt is a festering wound. We also have duties towards our spouses, children and other close family members. Living the life of a karma yogi, by performing all actions without being attached to results, is indeed a royal road to liberation.

Money lost can somehow be earned. But, time lost is lost forever. If we treat every day as a special day or a holy day, all our activities become sanctified. When we use our time wisely we live wisely, for time is life and life is nothing but time!

Bhagvad Gita: verse 2.64 But the self controlled man, moving among objects with senses under restraint, and free from attraction and aversion, attains to tranquility.

9th verse

CEILING ON DESIRES

To keep on filling
is not as good as stopping.
Overfilled, the cupped hands drip,
better to stop pouring.

Sharpen a blade too much
and its edge will soon be lost.
Fill your house with jade and gold
and it brings insecurity.
Puff yourself with honour and pride
and no one can save you from a fall.

Retire when the work is done;
this is the way to heaven.

According to a report I read sometime back, more suicides take place in Sweden, than anywhere else. Ironically, per capita income is also very high, if not the highest, there.

In nature, things have a beginning and also an end. Rivers do flood, but not all 365 days and not all through the ages. Nor do typhoons blow for ever. Earthquakes last for few seconds, although the devastation is colossal. The volcanoes spew flames like dragons, but also settle and cool down in the course of time.

In nature, everything settles down after some time. The only thing that never seems to settle down is man's desire for more. In fact, one desire fulfilled, creates in its place, ten more. Unfulfilled desire makes him angry and desperate. Thus, both fulfilled desire and unfulfilled desire create problems. Unfulfilled desires many times lead people to such frustration as to take their own life or destroy others. If self-destruction or suicide is one way of expressing frustration and the other extreme takes form of destroying others. These days, murderers can be hired. Wise men see the folly of this never-ending unrest and liken it to the chakravyooh (chakravyooh is a complicated formation of soldiers used in wars during the times of the Mahabharat). The story says that Arjuna's son Abhimanyu knew how to get into it but did not know how to come out, the result of which was he had to lose his life.

We are also in a similar predicament. We got into this huge trap called 'desires' but do not know how to come out of it. This quagmire of desire is so powerful, coming out is really a Herculean task.

**Sharpen a blade too much
and its edge will soon be lost.
Fill your house with jade and gold
and it brings insecurity.**

**Puff yourself with honour and pride
and no one can save you from a fall.**

As a school-going girl, in my anxiety to have a sharp pencil, I used to go on sharpening it. Though I could see it becoming smaller and smaller with every effort, my ignorant mind did not understand the problem. Some elders had to come to my rescue and tell me "this much only and no further!"

Being rich and famous seems to be a deadly combination. Film stars and celebrities have a tough time with the photographers and press. In fact, in the beginning of their journey towards popularity, they, many times run after media personalities so that they can be seen in the print or electronic media. But once they reach some level, they realize they have no private life. This scenario is very bad in many western countries. The celebrities are chased and hounded like wild animals by the paparazzi.

People in show business and other so called high-profile people, will go to any extent to keep themselves looking young and attractive all the time. These 'done up dolls', in this process of 'young forever' tag, go on crash-dieting, plastic (or is it drastic?) surgery etc. unmindful of the consequences in later years. Many times their lives end up with irreversible disease, drug-abuse, bankruptcy or suicide.

**Retire when the work is done;
this is the way to heaven.**

Liberation or 'way to heaven' is in not expecting anything in return for our labour. When a seed is sown, it will spring up some day or other by itself. We leave it to nature to do what needs to be done. Let us be like a gardener sowing seeds (doing actions) removing weeds (not attending to nor pursuing undesirable thoughts and actions) watering regularly (offering prayers) and waiting silently with eyes closed in reverence and awe for the mighty unseen forces working for us. Even a foolish man knows that if he has sown barley, he cannot harvest tomatoes. How then, did we, the intelligent, educated people forget this about the consequences of our actions?

Bhagavad Gita: verse 2.71: That man who lives devoid of longing, abandoning all desires, without the sense of "I" and "My", he attains to peace.

10th verse

THE ABLE ADMINSTRATOR

Carrying body and soul
and embracing the one,
can you avoid separation?

Can you let your body become
as supple as a newborn child's?
In the opening and shutting of heaven's gate,
can you play the feminine part?

Can you love your people
and govern your domain
without self-importance?

Giving birth and nourishing;
having, yet not possessing;
working, yet not taking credit;
leading without controlling or dominating.

**One who heeds this power
brings the Tao to this very earth.
This is the primal virtue.**

**Carrying body and soul
and embracing the one,
can you avoid separation?**

Am I the body having a soul? Or am I the soul having a body?

The body is temporary. It exists for a certain period of time. Without a body, no experience is possible. But soul is eternal. It is never born and it never dies. To experience Godliness, it takes form, especially the human form. Human beings are the privileged species amongst all creations, to raise themselves to such great heights as that of God.

Poet Hafiz says:

The illumined one
Who keeps
Seducing the formless into form
Had the charm to win my heart.
Only a Perfect one
Who is always
Laughing at the word two
Can make you know
of love!

"The illumined one"- Lao Tzu is referring to masters, or gurus. Their intense thirst for God makes Him take Form (Avatar).

Seducing the formless into form

Seducing refers to madhurava bhava(Divine Beloved) bhakthi. Hinduism allows the devotees to worship God according to their feelings. God can be my child, my parent, my master, friend, or even a foe. Every human feeling can be directed towards God.

In madhura bhava bhakthi, God is worshipped as a divine beloved. Meera, Andal and Lord Chaitanya Mahaprabhu had madhura bhava devotion. (whether the devotee is a male or a female is immaterial).

Bhaktha Prahlada (the child devotee) had such an intense devotion that it created the form of Lord Narasimha (Man-lion i.e half-lion half-man form). The little boy's father Hiranyakashyap denied the existence of God. Not only that, he had the audacity to proclaim himself as the almighty! Ironically, Hiranyakashyap, the man who denied the existence of God had been bestowed a boon (by Brahma, the Creator) according to which, he would never die by a man or an animal, neither inside or outside, neither on the land nor in air, neither in the day nor during night, neither by sharp or blunt weapons.

The nameless formless Tao is pulled by devotion and takes avatar (Form). Thus the Lord assumes the form of man-lion (Narasimha) and kills Hiranyakashyap by placing him on His own lap, during sandhya kal (dusk) sitting on the threshold and tore him by His claws.

Yad bhavo, tad bhavathi, as our feelings, so is our experience.

The attraction between a male and a female is mostly at the physical level. In many cases, after a few years, there is not much physical attraction or love between them. But, when a jeevatma (individual soul) longs to merge in the Paramatma(Universal Soul), devotion reaches its Himalayan peaks. Only egoless souls can reach this height. Even a slightest trace of ego will and can become a barrier.

Hafiz says; "only such as illumined' master who laughs at the word 'Two' (duality or dwaita) can win my heart." This one sentence is enough, I feel, to understand the glory of this master Hafiz, for he sees only "Oneness" !

**Can you let your body become
as supple as a newborn child's?
In the opening and shutting of heaven's gate,
can you play the feminine part?**

Body and mind are intrinsically connected. They are the obverse and reverse of the same coin. They influence each other and are inter-dependent.

Let us consider a case of a young robust man, enjoying excellent health. He goes for an interview and all of a sudden, fear of not being able to perform well in his interview grips him. Palpitation and sweating reflect his mental agitation. Many people under tension get headaches, diarrhea, etc. There is special type of fever called "examination fever". It miraculously subsides after the exams are over! Children are more prone to this type of fever.

Inference:- Mind has its effect on the body...

The same Mr. X referred to above, one day over-boozes. Now this healthy man's gait is affected. He staggers and his speech becomes incoherent. He behaves like an idiot. What happened to him?

The 'stuff' inside his body is in control of his mind

Inference;- Body has its effect on the mind

Simple arithmetic indeed!

This is the main reason for advocating satvic food (vegetarian food that are non spicy and not very oily) for any sadhak.(spiritual aspirant)

Children are beautiful because they are innocent. The mind is not tarnished by the world. If a person can retain his innocence, (purity of mind) his body will be beautiful like that of a child. Many saints and sages develop strong auras around themselves and their faces literally glow. I read somewhere that Lord Buddha had such a glow. And so did Yogi Aurobindo.

"In opening and shutting of heaven's gate, can you play the feminine part?"

Heaven is indicative of good life. If it shuts its door on us, we suffer. It is easy to be charitable, sacrificing, and philanthropic if we are well off. But, can we be sacrificing when we have less? The feminine aspect of a person is selfless love, and sacrifice is the spontaneous reaction of this tender feeling.

Blessed indeed are people who have less but give more!

Can you love your people
and govern your domain
without self-importance ?

Giving birth and nourishing;
having, yet not possessing;
working, yet not taking credit;
leading without controlling or dominating.

One who heeds this power
brings the Tao to this very earth.
This is the primal virtue.

People in power become arrogant and conceited and misuse their power in different ways. They keep themselves above all and tend to become very selfish. "Make hay while the sun shines". This adage suits them very well for they want to amass wealth while still in power. They become very egoistic for they have some group of people dancing to their tunes. Such people have an axe to grind. Once the person in power is dethroned, these people will just disperse and disappear! Such opportunists are worse than prostitutes. Prostitutes sell only their bodies. But, these unscrupulous people sell their soul. Can there be redemption for such fall from grace?

As against this, is the man of Tao...a man of God. He works for the people and yet claims no credit thereof. All his resources are for serving others. He leads a simple and frugal life. Such people do not try to control or dominate over others for the truth that 'only God is the master... and all of us are here to serve others' has dawned on him.

The nameless, formless one has to be pulled to this earth by our 'primal virtue' which is pure selfless love for all creations of God. Even if one person or thing is left out, love is not complete. The other virtues like kindness, forgiveness, equanimity are just the off-springs of this 'primal' virtue.

Bhagvad Gita: 6.30

He who sees Me in all things and sees all things in Me, he never becomes separated from Me, nor do I become separated from him.

11th verse

EMPTINESS IS ALL ENCOMPASSING

Thirty spokes converge upon a single hub;
it is on the hole in the centre that
the use of the cart hinges;

Shape clay into a vessel;
it is the space within that makes it useful.
Carve fine doors and windows,
but the room is useful in its emptiness.

The usefulness of what is
depends on what is not.

An empty cup can be filled with something. Similarly, a room is useful because of its emptiness. Emptiness/space is needed so that things can occupy that void. We can put our sofa sets and dining sets because there is space. The concept of Great Emptiness is skillfully explained by the master craftsman Lao Tzu to explain the inexplicable Tao. This is the essence of Tao Teh Ching.

A room cluttered with too many things restricts our movement. Going into the forest and wilderness is one way of searching for space. In fact, losing ourselves in nature replenishes the energy we lose by constant association with too many things and too many people. Some need solitude for recovering from tragedy; be it physical, financial or emotional. They scream; "leave me alone'. How much ever we love a person, if he or she clings to us 24 hours, we will be bored. Space is needed: distance is needed. People going into depression, stand near the window and stare at the sky, the total emptiness. There are many ways to create space. The paradox is, it cannot be created or destroyed.

Our mind is full of thoughts. Many of us have pre-conceived ideas about certain people. This prejudice is also some kind of cluttering the mind. Thoughts many times are termed as chain of thoughts. The function of a chain is to restrict our movement. Thus our own thoughts, especially the negative ones, chain us, bind us, blind us and we blame all the stars in the heaven for our misfortune. Hence, Dr.Wayne Dyer says, "Change your thoughts- Change your life".

A person who meditates regularly experiences thoughtlessness, at least for some time. Thus, space is created between thoughts. New, creative ideas burst forth in such thoughtless awareness. Osho calls it 'no mind meditation'. If we meditate regularly, we will experience great tranquility that just over-flows.

Though cells are tightly packed, still there is some space between them, which we call as intra-cellular space. During pranayama, one experiences this 'void' between two breaths. This is the reason pranayama is advocated by many masters for spiritual development.

A person who lives 'I, me and myself,' are full of 'themselves'. They tend to become selfish for they seldom have space for others to walk into their lives. Many times, they live a solitary life and this self-imposed alienation takes its toll as they grow old.

12th verse

HUNTERS WILL BE EXHAUSTED

The five colors blind the eye.
The five tones deafen the ear.
The five flavors dull the taste.
The chase and the hunt craze people's minds.

Wasting energy to obtain rare objects
only impedes one's growth.

The master observes the world
but trusts his inner vision.
He allows things to come and go.
He prefers what is within to what is without.

Colour is not to be understood as 'shades or tints'. The 'five colors' are the five sense organs whose demand never seem to end. These insatiable thirsts for external things blind a man and force him into many unworthy and undesirable actions.

We fall a prey to our five senses. We sadly mistake that by giving in to our sense gratification, we can satisfy them. Unfortunately, just its opposite is the truth! The more we get, the more we crave. It is like putting off fire by adding fuel to it.

Our ancestors were hunters. They went hunting mainly for food. In spite of having our food on our table without much effort, still our primitive instinct of chasing and hunting seem to be intact - for we are still chasing...not animals, but things to satisfy our insatiable demand of our five senses.

We see people working from morning to night trying to get more and more money. There comes the next worry of how to protect the wealth from enemies. Many times the enemies are disguised as greedy children or other close relatives. For some reason, if he is unable to earn, the very same people for whom he worked all his life, do not care for him anymore. Old age, disease and other physical infirmities add to his woes. Life thus wasted, the one wish the poor man has is to rest in eternal peace!

An atheist wanted to have some fun with a master, and asked him about the distance between himself and God. The master softly replied; 'the longer the list, farther away he was from God.'

Moral: let us shorten our distance.

We are given this previous life for self-realization. Unfortunately, many of us spend our lives in collecting things and amassing wealth which impedes our spiritual growth for which we are here on this earth.

**The master observes the world
but trusts his inner vision.
He allows things to come and go.
He prefers what is within to what is without.**

Lao Tzu says that a master observes the world. Thus, a master becomes a witness to whatever is happening. This witnessing is the main crux of vipassana meditation. Such a person who has mastered this art of witnessing, experiences inner vision or aatma gyan. Like a person near the sea shore observing the tides coming and going, he also witnesses the happenings of the world.

It does not need any intelligence to know that we can do nothing to the sea except observing it.

Bhagavad Gita: verse 5.22: Since enjoyments that are contact-born are parents of misery alone, and with beginning and end, O son of Kunti (Arjuna), a wise man does not seek pleasure in them.

13th verse

FLATTENED THINGS DO NOT FALL

Favour and disgrace seem alarming.
High status greatly afflicts your person.

Why are favour and disgrace alarming?
Seeking favour is degrading:
alarming when it is gotten,
alarming when it is lost.

Why does high status greatly afflict your person?
The reason we have a lot of trouble
is that we have selves.
If we had no selves,
what trouble would we have?

Man's true self is eternal,
yet he thinks, I am this body and will soon die.
If we have no body, what calamities can we have?
One who sees himself as everything
is fit to be guardian of the world.

pramila iyer

**One who loves himself as everyone
is fit to be teacher of the world.**

Seeking 'favour' is like handling a double-edged weapon. To be in good books, we go out of our way to please the person. The other person becomes more important which means less self-respect. A person having less self-respect falls from Grace. Self-respect should not be confused with egoism. To receive favors, one tends to use flattery very liberally. This boosts the ego of the person thus flattered. In due course it becomes an addiction. He wants people to surround him and say all good things about him. Naturally there is a price. Price can be in terms of money, increment, promotion, or getting a seat in school or college, and much more. To please these people, the flattered man has to use flattery of another kind to people above him. Thus, they all get trapped by each other.

Seeking favors is like a two edged sword. When granted, we are bound to our donor… if refused, we become angry. Receiving makes us feel small; non-receiving makes us angry. This is the two-edged sword. This is the deadly dance of the ego. It needs constant food like Bakasura (mythological demon who would go on eating everything). Ego is the root cause of all the problems of the world.

**Man's true self is eternal,
yet he thinks, I am this body and will soon die.
If we have no body, what calamities can we have?
One who sees himself as everything
is fit to be guardian of the world.
One who loves himself as everyone
is fit to be teacher of the world.**

There is an individual ego, which says 'I am the best'. Religious ego says: 'our religion is the best' (hence destroy others). To some extent, the individual ego helps us to grow, but the religious ego's only motto is 'kill them all and come back alone'.

All the troubles we experience are because of possessing a body. With death the body will not exist. Since all the problems belong to the body and death will make us free, why do we all fear death? The Master must be amused by our fear of death, and at the same time, in his compassion, is reassuring us about our eternal life and that there is no need to fear death either of our selves or our dear ones.

"One who loves himself as everyone"

Or should it be.

"one who loves everyone as his own self"?

Well, the first sentence is the translation available from Dr.Wayne's book.

I was confused for quite some time. The second sentence looked more appropriate. Then suddenly it dawned on me as to the correctness of the first statement;

I love my parents

I love my husband

I love my relatives and friends

Did I ever say I love myself? If I did not have love (for myself) how can I give it to somebody? I must, in the first place have it, before I can give it to others.

"One who sees himself as everything".

I think it is the most beautiful sentence containing the whole essence of advaita philosophy. This is all expansive empathy, like a river flowing and quenching the thirst of everyone without reservation or distinction. He sees himself in a humble grass to a huge mountain. He sees himself in people belonging to other race, religion and culture. Thus, he knows to respect everything around him, for he has become one with them. When he helps somebody, he knows he is helping his own self and none else. When such as understanding comes, where is the question of seeking reward? How can such a person ever hurt anybody? In fact, his love energy is so high that even animals instinctively experience it.

Such a man is a universal parent…a universal teacher.. like Buddha, Krishna, Jesus or Osho!

With such parents, everyone feels safe and protected.

Bhagvad Gita: 12.18 and 12.9 (combined)

He who is same to friend and foe, and also in honour and dishonor; who is the same in heat and cold, and in pleasure and pain; who is free from attachment; to whom censure and praise are equal; who is silent, content with anything, homeless, steady minded, full of devotion – that man is dear to Me.

Bhagvad Gita; verse; 15.5 Free from pride and delusion, with evil of attachment conquered, ever dwelling in the Self, with desires completely receded, liberated from pairs of opposites known as pleasure and pain, the undeluded reach that Goal Eternal(liberation).

14th Verse

FROM FORM TO FORMLESS

That which cannot be seen is called invisible.
That which cannot be heard is called inaudible.
That which cannot be held is called intangible,
These three cannot be defined;
therefore, they are merged as one

Each of these three is subtle for description.
By intuition you can see it,
hear it and feel it.
Then the unseen,
unheard,
and untouched
are present as one.

Its rising brings no dawn,
its setting no darkness;
it goes on and on, unnameable,
returning into nothingness.

Approach it and there is no beginning;
follow it and there is no end.
You cannot know it, but you can be it,
at ease in your own life.

Discovering how things have always been
Brings one into harmony with the Way.

We perceive the world through our five senses. The five senses belong to our body. Many times we are lost in our thoughts. We are at that time not using our organs of perception, but our mind. Mind always oscillates between past and future and misses the present.

Tao (The Supreme Being) is eternal. It, therefore, has no past and no future. It is always 'is'...always in the present.

Present also means gift. The greatest gift we can give ourselves is living in the present. As a driver of a vehicle uses the rear view mirror only occasionally to veer the vehicle properly, let us learn the art of 'looking back' (past)only when needed.

God is described as Light by some; to some it is Life; and to some it is sound "om".

If God is light, then what is darkness?

If God is life, then what is death?

If God is sound, why glorify silence as a pathway to realization?

The answer seems simple; God or Tao is everything that is and can be.

Its rising brings no dawn,
its setting no darkness;

**it goes on and on, unnameable,
returning into nothingness.**

We see the sun rising and setting every day. Does it really rise? Does it really set? We know it neither rises nor sets. It appears so, because the earth where we all live is moving. A spectacular optical illusion for all of us indeed! We can either enjoy or ignore. The choice is ours.
Spirituality and science thus walk together.

**Approach it and there is no beginning;
follow it and there is no end.
You cannot know it, but you can be it,
at ease in your own life.**

**Discovering how things have always been
Brings one into harmony with the Way.**

Sai Baba of Puttaparthy says:
Don't walk in front...I may not follow you
Don't walk behind me.. you will not catch me
walk by my side.

Walking in front; (means) : putting conditions...(I tell you what to do...I lead...you follow.(just like a command...)
Walking behind; (means) : begging for favours (beggary is unbecoming of devotee)
Walking by the side is; (means) implicit and innocent trust (child like)
Children always walk by the side of parents. The parents in their love for their children, walk according to their pace.

It is natural for a child to trust the parents implicitly. If a child holds father's hand, the grip may not be tight enough; but, if the father holds him, the child is safe. Let Him hold our hands.

When we develop this kind of deep trust in Tao, the source of everything, our life is taken care of.

Bhagvad Gita verse no.12.3 and 12.4 (combined)

But those who, worship the Imperishable, the Indefinable, the Unmanifested, the Omnipresent, the Unthinkable, the Unchangeable, the Immovable, the Eternal – having subdued all the senses, even-minded everywhere, engaged in the welfare of all being – verily they reach only Myself.

15th verse

BE A GUEST EVEN IN YOUR OWN HOME

The ancient masters were profound and subtle.
Their wisdom was unfathomable.
There is no way to describe it.
One can only describe them vaguely by their
appearance.

Watchful, like men crossing a winter stream.
Alert, like men aware of danger.
Simple as uncarved wood.
Hollow like caves.
Yielding, like ice about to melt.
Amorphous, like muddy water. (lacking a specific
shape, shapeless, indefinable, unrecognizable.

But the muddiest water clears
as it is stilled.
And out of that stillness
life arises.

He who keeps the Tao does not want to be full.
But precisely because he is never full,
he can remain like a hidden sprout
And does not rush to early ripening.

Lao Tzu speaks of the ancient masters as:

1) Watchful like men crossing the winter stream

The winter stream sometimes has ice floating, which can mislead a person about the depth of the water. Hence, he treads carefully. This refers to his actions which are performed with great care and deliberation.

2) Alert like men aware of danger

Danger need not come in the form of wild animals. We have men who are cunning like a fox, dangerous like cobra and unpredictable like a wild elephant. In spite of such challenges, he knows Tao is all inclusive and as such, a man of Tao is careful about every work he does weighing the pros and cons of his actions.

In Bhagavad Gita, the Lord says that a yogi never sleeps. Lao Tzu is describing such a master in many different ways.

3) Simple as uncarved wood

If the wood is carved, it attains just one form. But the uncarved wood has all the infinite potentials hidden in it, yet humble and simple in its countenance. A true master living in harmony with existence lives in fullness, for he knows that in the universe things happen according to some Great Plan. He performs all actions as an offering to the Great Tao, the source of 10,000 things. Desireless and unattached, he roams freely, contended with what he has, and committed to what he does.

4)   Hollow like caves

Anybody can take shelter in a cave. A man of Tao like a cave, will give shelter (refuge) to anybody who cares to come to him, animals included!

5)   Yielding like ice about to melt.

Ice melts with our every touch. A man of God is touched by the plight of people around him, for so great is his care and concern for people. Ice looks solid, which we know is not its truth. A saint at times looks very stoic and cold, but in his heart he has over-whelming compassion.

6)   Amorphous like muddy water

Rigidity of thinking is a subtle form of ego. True saints are ever flowing with creation. Water flows very freely whereas muddy water is slow in flowing. Free flowing can lead to impulsive actions, for which, one might have to regret later on. Lao Tzu describes a man immersed in Tao as 'amorphous like muddy water'. Not just actions, even his speech are measured. This shows his mastery over his own self. Words thrown carelessly and actions done on an impulse can lead to unwanted problems in our lives.

Life is like a river. A wise man flows with it and thus saves his own energy. Only fools go against the stream, and end up exhausted and defeated.

He who keeps the Tao does not want to be full.
But precisely because he is never full,
he can remain like a hidden sprout
And does not rush to early ripening.

Lao Tzu says that a man of Tao has no need for external things to make him happy. He prefers to live in obscurity. Like a seed hidden in the ground gently sprouting, he blooms yet remains hidden. He lets nature to take its own course in making that little plant available for others.

A peacock dances when rain bearing clouds cover the sky. Whether people watch it not, it does not care. Dancing is its nature. Similarly, a man of Tao remains hidden from the public gaze.

Bhagavad Gita: verse 17.16: Serenity of mind, kindliness, silence, self-control, honesty of motive- this is called as mental austerity.

16th VERSE

ETERNAL LAW OF LIFE

Become totally empty.
Let your heart be at peace.
Amidst the rush of worldly comings and goings,
observe how endings become beginnings.

Things flourish, each by each,
only to return to the Source.....
to what is and what is to be.

To return to the root is to find peace.
To find peace is to fulfill one's destiny.
To fulfill one's destiny is to be constant.
To know the constant is called insight.
Not knowing this cycle
leads to eternal disaster.

Knowing the constant gives perspective.
This perspective is impartial.
Impartiality is the highest nobility;
the highest nobility is Divine.

Being Divine, you will be at one with the Tao.
Being at one with the Tao is eternal.
This way is everlasting,
not endangered by physical death.

Change is the only constant in this world. Child grows into an adult and then to an old man and one day becomes one with nature – his final journey may end in the cemetery or funeral pyre. Early childhood is the only time when he is free from worries. As a student, he is worried about the marks, as an employee, about his performance in his office. After marriage, he is expected to be good husband or son-in-law. Then, it is his children he has to please. Thus, his entire life is spent in tension and worries.

In Indian tradition, all poojas /chanting or any other spiritual activity concludes with "om shanthi, shanthi shanthihi". It is a belief in many religious customs, that whatever is repeated thrice happens. When we chant 'shanthi', which means 'peace' that is also attained/ attainable, for God is 'Shanthi Swaroopa' which means embodiment of peace.

A spiritual aspirant has to overcome many obstacles, which are enumerated as follows:

1) adi daivikam …obstacles from five elements or nature: like earth-quakes, flooding etc.

2) adi bhoutikam obstacles from our environment: wars, riots, etc.(man made)

3) adi atmikam: obstacles from our own selves: lethargy, procrastination, lack of enthusiasm, constant criticism, fear(mostly imaginary) etc.

Solution to the third problem is in our hands. Most of us check our e-mails every day. At least one day we can check our own mails. What does my mail say? Was I rude? Did I lose my temper for no reason? Am I postponing my true happiness by going after illusory happiness? Who trapped me? My parents? My husband?...none of them. I trapped myself because of my expectation. I wanted certain things in my life to happen the way I want it to happen. I chained myself and was holding God or the stars in which I was born to be responsible. So I had to do a hundred things to please them.

I understood my folly, and I made a conscious choice, and in that freedom of choice, I share my thoughts with whoever reads this text.

Lao Tzu says:
Impartiality is the highest nobility
Impartiality towards other people is just the tip of the ice berg of life.
Can we have equanimity in a calamity?
Can we remain unperturbed in loss?

Lao Tzu says that "impartiality is the highest nobility". Sometimes even parents, who are supposed to be impartial, show some partiality amongst their own children. A sick child is given more importance and naturally the other children feel neglected. An obedient child is preferred than to a rebellious one. These qualities are human weaknesses. Sometimes traditions also play a major role in our lives. One of the traditions followed in India is that the parents live with their sons. As grand-parents they pamper the children of their daughters more than the children of their sons. The reason being in Indian household parents live with their sons and married daughters come only occasionally. This attitude sometimes takes its toll and creates bitterness in the family. Lao Tzu says "this is just the tip of an ice berg"... much more is there in store for us!

Can we remain just a witness to whatever happens around us? Can I remain unperturbed if there is some great tragedy like heavy financial loss, or sudden or untimely death of a loved one? There is no answer to these questions for all of us react differently to situations of life. The important thing is to come back to our stability after some calamity. If we can achieve even this much, it will be great victory to many of us.

Will not that lead to inaction on our part?

We all know that everything comes to an end. Losses come to an end and so does profit. A man of wisdom with this understanding of cyclic nature of things remains a witness to life.

All these questions that arise in our mind have answers in Bhagvad Gita.

Bhagvad Gita: verse 2.38.

The Lord says: Having made pleasure and pain, gain and loss, conquest and defeat, the same, engage thou then in battle. So shalt thou incur no sin.

When such equanimity is attained (which is attainable) profit brings no happiness...loss brings no unhappiness. Such yogi has crossed the bridge.

17th Verse

SAINT IS SELF-EFFACING

With the greatest leader above them,
people barely know one exists.
Next comes one whom they love and praise.
Next comes one, whom they fear.
Next comes one, whom they despise and defy.

When a leader trusts no one,
no one trusts him.

The great leader speaks little.
He never speaks carelessly.
He works without self-interest
and leaves no trace.
When all is finished, the people say,
"We did it ourselves."

With the greatest leader above them,
people barely know one exists.

I feel this refers to the Satya yuga described in the Hindu scriptures. Satya means 'truth'. This era was the era of the 'greatest truth'… the Supreme Being in all its glory and splendour where the inhabitants were so immersed in 'Truth' that they had become one with the 'Truth'. Here everything was immaculate, most glorious, incomparable, pristine energy.

Next comes one whom they love and praise,

To my mind, it refers to "Threta yuga". We have many avatars during this period. The Gods and deities were loved and revered by people.

The master Lao Tzu is referring to personal deities/ spiritual heads according to one's beliefs. Many rites are rituals to appease their personal Gods/deities.

Next comes one, whom they fear.
Next comes one, whom they despise and defy.

When a leader trusts no one,
No one trusts him

History of the world is full of horrendous stories of some religious organizations imparting training even to children to kill people of other religions. If anybody opposes them, even if they belong to their own faith, will be killed. These killing machines, like cancer, have entered all over the world. Such religious organizations thrive on creating fear amongst people. These lost souls are in the last rung of the spiritual ladder. They have lost everything; lost love, lost compassion, lost respect and all that is humane. Such terror machines are not wanted even by people of their own faith. Instead of enjoying the abundance they hide themselves in trenches and tunnels.

From this original state of fullness, the consciousness goes down and then come the rulers who are not loved and revered for they have become very selfish and ruthless. They visit slums and make promises which are never kept. Such rulers have a group of people hanging around them as a dog waiting at the dining table of the master for some crumbs. Not that they are faithful like dogs...neither such a leader will trust his group nor will the group trust him for their relationship is based on mutual benefit system. Selfishness will not allow such rulers to trust anyone for they themselves have been not trust-worthy!

The great leader speaks little,
He never speaks carelessly
He works without self-interest
And leaves no trace.
When all is finished,
The people say"
"we did it ourselves."

As a total contrast, is the ruler who speaks little. 'Speaking little' does not mean inadequacy of his vocabulary. Here the meaning is he does not make false promises. Since he keeps up his words, people trust him. Trust is always an all encompassing feeling. Rulers with refined consciousness make people feel a part of everything that happens. People take responsibility for the welfare of their kingdom and join hands to create a 'heaven on earth'.

Bhagvad Gita: 18.51 Endued with a pure intellect; subduing the body and the senses forth fortitude; *relinquishing sound and such other sense-object; abandoning attraction and hatred.

(*relinquishing sound; speaks only that which is necessary)

18th Verse

AVOID ARTIFICIAL GOODNESS

When the greatness of the Tao is present,
action arises from one's own heart.
When the greatness of the Tao is absent,
action comes from the rules
of "kindness and justice."

If you need rules to be kind and just,
if you <u>act</u> virtuous,
This is a sure sign that virtue is absent.
Thus we see the great hypocrisy.

When kinship falls into discord,
piety and rites of devotion arise.
When the country falls into chaos,
official loyalists will appear;
patriotism is born.

**When the greatness of the Tao is present,
action arises from one's own heart.
When the greatness of the Tao is absent,
action comes from the rules
of "kindness and justice."**

Lao Tzu's words hit us like swords. He says if you are kind, just and virtuous, you have none of them!

After the initial shock, I deeply pondered over his statement.

I was born in a middle class family. Our friends and relatives belonged to the upper strata ...economically at least. As we could not afford much of gold, we wore gold plated ornaments. We wanted to tell silently that we were equally rich. (because we were not!)

**If you need rules to be kind and just,
if you <u>act</u> virtuous,
This is a sure sign that virtue is absent.
Thus we see the great hypocrisy.**

Every religion preaches kindness and justice. It is like the gold plated ornaments I wore. Think over it!

Tithing or charity is also advocated by many religious leaders promising the people that it will open the gates to heaven. All the dos and don'ts of religion are to frighten people of hell or to lure them to a place called 'heaven'. The charity given, in such cases, is not from the heart. Such acts of charity can never stand on par with a heart that wants to share its wealth, without being told to do so!

Why do we have so many places of worship to worship? Worship is reverence for the Almighty. Are not the rivers, seas, mountains, forests, wind almighty...powerful? Air when becomes a cyclone, can we stop it? The water in the pot quenches our thirst. If it takes its gigantic form and sweeps you in its torrents, how much can be saved? If earth quake hits, who is going to help us? The government...the politicians...?

There is no special place for 'God'. Every place is special.. every creation is special ..I am special and so are you!

Every country has its rules and regulations. When they are broken, the law enforcing authorities come pouncing. Unfortunately, money and power over-power these people, and thus the law-protectors become law breakers. Because of this, many criminals go scot free and people trust the law no more.

Only two things rule over the world at present;1. Money...2. Power. Honesty and sincerity are the two words found only in dictionaries. Satyameva jayate; 'only truth triumphs' we were told when we were in school. It is very unfortunate that only money and power triumph now. Do I re-phrase it by saying "Asatya meva jayate."?..untruth only triumphs ? Hope not..If all of us get together with noble ideas we can create a happy new world.

When kinship falls into discord,
piety and rites of devotion arise.
When the country falls into chaos,
official loyalists will appear;
patriotism is born.

India is undergoing some dramatic developments. People have finally woken up to the hard realities of the inefficiency and unscrupulous attitudes of politicians. They want to bring back the glory of Ram Rajya. (godly governance). Patriotism has become a mass movement in India now. The many, otherwise aloof, spiritual gurus have also joined hands with common people to make this birthing process smoother. They touch the heart of the people and a ray of hope is gleaming for this great country!

Lao Tzu seems to have foreseen the events of the world and I feel if we walk on his path, we will create heaven on earth.

19th Verse

IGNORANCE TO INNOCENCE

Give up sainthood, renounce wisdom,
and it will be a hundred times better for everyone.
Throw away morality and justice
and people will do the right thing.
Throw away industry and profit
and there will no thieves.

All of these are outward forms alone;
they are not sufficient in themselves.

It is more important
to see the simplicity,
to realize one's true nature,
to cast off selfishness
and temper desire.

People work hard, sacrificing their time and energy to become more and more richer. One fine day, a man thinks of giving up his life of pleasure and plenty and joins some ashram seeking a 'guru'. In due course a few things change.. like the way he dresses, his food habits, etc. But deep down the person is not much different. This is the reason why so many religious institutions are hounded by the police and the press. There also have been murders and rapes!. Where is the sainthood then?

**It is more important
to see the simplicity,
to realize one's true nature,
to cast off selfishness
and temper desire.**

This is the reason Lao-tzu is asking us to give up sainthood. Instead, become a 'parent of the world' and parenthood is never tired of doing its best. Sharing comes naturally.

When there is 'parenthood' the question of amassing wealth does not arise. We, as parents to our biological children, do not mind to do any amount of sacrifice. This sacrifice is because of the feeling 'my children'. There is no need for any body to tell us to do our best for them. This is what 'simplicity' is...no external force...no external threats (to perform our duties)...no rules and regulations.... we simply do it! Such 'parents of the world' always do their best for they believe in the adage 'vasudeva kutumbakam... the whole world is one family'. Just imagine a world where everybody works for everybody! Thus everybody will live a life of glory.

Bhagavad Gita: verse 5.25: With imperfections exhausted, doubts dispelled, senses controlled, engaged in the good of all beings, the Rishies (men of right vision and renunciation i.e.saintly people) obtain absolute freedom.

20th Verse

INDIFFERENCE IS THE DIFFERENCE

Give up learning and you will be free from all your cares.
What is the difference between yes and no?
What is the difference between good and evil?

Must I fear what others fear?
Should I fear desolation when there is abundance?
Should I fear darkness when there is light everywhere?

In spring, some go to the park and climb the terrace,
but I alone am drifting, not knowing where I am.
Like a newborn babe before it learns to smile,
I am alone, without a place to go.

Most people have too much; I alone seem to be missing something.
Mine is indeed the mind of ignoramus
in its unadulterated simplicity.
I am but a guest in this world.

While others rush about to get things done,
I accept what is offered.
I alone seem foolish, earning little, spending less.

Other people strive for fame; I avoid limelight,
preferring to be left alone.
Indeed, I seem like an idiot; no mind, no worries.

I drift like a wave on the ocean.
I blow as aimless as the wind.

All men settle down in their grooves;
I alone am stubborn and remain outside.
But wherein I am most different from other is
in knowing to take sustenance from the great Mother!

Give up learning and you will be free from all your cares.
What is the difference between yes and no?
What is the difference between good and evil?

This paragraph comes as a shock, mocking at us for all our efforts, energy and time we have spent in acquiring knowledge and possessing wealth. Even an illiterate man tries to learn how to carry heavy loads on his head for he makes faster strides so that he can unload himself in a minimum possible time. Every knowledge mundane or spiritual if performed to prove 'oneself' better than the rest. When we are 'the best', where is the need to prove something? When we trust ourselves to be great produced by the Great, where is the question of proving 'greatness'? If you are not 'great' how are you ever going to prove that which you are not? Both the attempts are futile by themselves... This is the wisdom hidden between these lines.

Must I fear what others fear?
Should I fear desolation when there is abundance?
Should I fear darkness when there is light everywhere?

Negative feelings, thoughts and ideas seem to be more powerful than positive vibrations, for somehow this energy is transmitted more easily. We know how rumours spread panic and create total chaos. People go on acquiring and accumulating things because of fear of the future. One seed does not produce only one fruit. It produces a tree which in turn can produce many fruits, and many more seeds!!

This is the message of abundance of creation. Ignorant people do not understand about the power of nature which is always Abundance. Ignorance is the darkness. In darkness, we want to hold to whatever is available...even if it were a snake!

When we understand the abundance available all around us, fear will fear us. It will have no place in our lives.

In spring, some go to the park and climb the terrace,
but I alone am drifting, not knowing where I am.
Like a newborn babe before it learns to smile,
I am alone, without a place to go.

A new born babe has no likes or dislikes. It has no free will. It has no plans for future and no position to acquire. Its innocence is captivating but it is unaware of its own greatness. Not knowing its own greatness adds to its greatness. They say old age is second childhood It can be, if there is spontaneous smile and care-free innocence. Not having teeth or almost going down on four legs...maybe three, with a walking stick to support, cannot be called as the 'second childhood'.

> **Most people have too much; I alone seem to be missing something.**
> **Mine is indeed the mind of ignoramus**
> **in its unadulterated simplicity.**
> **I am but a guest in this world.**
> **While others rush about to get things done,**
> **I accept what is offered.**
> **I alone seem foolish, earning little, spending less.**

Lao-tzu says he is a 'guest'. A guest is expected not to expect when he stays with his friends or relatives. He cannot demand anything in particular and should feel obliged and happy with whatever he gets.

Likes and dislikes lead to disappointment to the guest, and displeasure to his host. If the guest has no likes and dislikes, people will be happy to have him around. Lao Tzu's humility in all its glory is revealed when he says "mine is indeed the mind of ignoramus". 'I alone seem foolish'. This is a total contrast to people who claim to be gurus boasting about their 'difficult sadhana' or 'journey' and how God chose them as special messengers from among the millions!

> **Other people strive for fame; I avoid limelight, preferring to be left alone.**
> **Indeed, I seem like an idiot; no mind, no worries.**

Intelligent people seem to worry more than people with less intelligence. The left side of their brain is more active than the creative right brain. Too much of intelligence will not allow a person to enjoy even a flower. He will want to know what chemicals it contains, what are the ideal conditions for its growth etc. The flower in his hands fades away, and he wonders now as to why it withered away! He lost his chance of enjoying the flower when it was alive. Now, only the memory exists. Memories are ghosts and ghosts are dead-beings ! If you want to enjoy a flower, throw away your mind which constantly bombards us with all sorts of questions. That is why Laotzu says; no mind...no worries.!

Seeking name and fame is one way of silent screaming born out of lack of self-worth. Posing for photographs with a sapling in one hand and a water jug in another, after destroying acres and acres of forests by being a party to unscrupulous elements in destroying them, will make others hate them.

There are people who contribute to the betterment of the world in their own way, because they want to do it. It will not be out of place if I mention here about a woman from Kenya (Africa) who introduced the idea of planting of trees way back in 1976. She assisted women in planting more than 20 million trees on their farms, schools, churches, etc. She did not do it for name or fame. It was her strong sense of duty that made her do it. To me, she is a true parent of the world discussed earlier.

I drift like a wave on the ocean.
I blow as aimless as the wind.
All men settle down in their grooves;

I alone am stubborn and remain outside.
But wherein I am most different from other is
in knowing to take sustenance from the great
Mother!

Lao Tzu's love for nature is revealed in many places. His wisdom

flows like water...

makes our ego melt like ice....

captivates us like the fresh snow.....

caresses us like the gentle breeze....

sweeps us like the mountain stream ...

drowns us like the mighty ocean ....

His deep love and reverence for nature makes him a great teacher using minimum words to explain maximum about 'living in freedom'.

The five elements find their places in his verses as in a delicate tapestry...intricate...intimate...interwoven...inter-dependent ! A person with so much reverence to nature calling it 'mother' will surely be nourished by it. When you revere something, you will do your utmost to protect and preserve them in the best way possible. Nature, whether we revere or not, has no distinction. But the difference is very visible in the case of LaoTzu. He uses them as we all do but the comparison ends there, for he uses them judiciously putting his total trust about things happening according to some superior, invisible force....the Great Tao!.

A great master enjoys freedom....

Only a free person can be great master!

21st Verse

MICROCOSM TO MACROCOSM

The greatest virtue is to follow the Tao and the Tao
alone.
The Tao is elusive and intangible.
Although formless and intangible,
it gives rise to form.
Although vague and elusive,
it gives rise to shapes.
Although dark and obscure,
it is the spirit, the essence,
the life breath of all things.
Throughout the ages, its name has been preserved
in order to recall the beginning of all things.
How do I know the ways of all things at the
beginning?
I look inside myself and see what is within me.

The idea of 'mystery' with which Lao Tzu started
in the first chapter is re-opened here. As we can never

describe electricity, words fail to express the origin of the limitless power behind the 10,000 things we see all around us. Whenever we want to create something, we need the material, and the intelligence and somebody behind it to create. What material was used in creating the cosmos? What is the intelligence behind it? Who was that somebody? These questions can never be answered by a scientist because he is always looking for something tangible, something outside of himself.

Hinduism says: The material, the intelligence and 'somebody' is one and the same!. This power or energy or shakthi in Sanskrit thus becomes the 'mool karan' or 'original cause' for creation. What becomes elusive to even brilliant brains, reveals itself to people who go inwards.

Lao tzu's love for nature has been described in various chapters. God and creation...the material...the intelligence and the 'somebody' can be explained in a humble way if we look into a silk worm. The cocoon is created by it's own body and wraps about itself with it and goes to deep slumber. After some days, it flies away as a butter fly fluttering its glorious wings. If we have the vision to look beyond appearances, we will see what only a few people can see: the invisible!'.

We can 'follow' something which has a form. We can also 'follow' some concepts or ideas or ideology by putting them into practice. When Tao is neither tangible nor any particular ideology as its quality, how to 'follow' Tao? Tao is all pervading, ever present principle of life. It is all that is, yet it is none of them. Hindus call it 'neti' 'neti'...not this... not this... Then what is it? It is the 'all-inclusive' power that holds the million galaxies in their places.

How do I know the ways of all things at the beginning?
I look inside myself and see what is within me.

Hindu scriptures say that, 'If you know That, you will know every thing. In other words, knowing That by which every thing is known. Ironically, to know That, you have to know yourself. How to know myself? By observing myself.... sitting and silently observing our thoughts and whatever feelings we experience as we watch them, from head to feet. As in any mundane achievement, spiritual achievements also requires patience, perseverance and practice. As the same electricity cooks my food (by heating), cools my food (by preservation in a refrigerator), gives life working through some apparatus in an hospital and kills a man on the execution chair...every work is done with the very same principle. When all pairs of opposites merge as one, the invisible One, Tao, as we have been referring to, will lead us to unconditional joy of living!

Religion can give only glimpses of the glory of God. It is just a small window to lure you outside. Once in the open, where is need for any window?

Bhagvad Gita: 9.4.All this world is pervaded by Me in My unmanifested form: all beings exist in Me...but I do not dwell in them.

A little explanation to the above shloka will give a better understanding. Let us take a simple analogy. I have one box which needs to be covered. The cover has to be greater than the box. If I have ten boxes, naturally I will need a much bigger one to cover them.

The cover, thus, has to be greater that what it covers. This is the meaning of 'all beings dwell in Me...but I do not dwell in them.'

22nd Verse

SECRET REVEALED

The flexible are preserved unbroken.
The bent become straight.
The empty are filled.
The exhausted become renewed.
The poor are enriched.
The rich are confounded.

Therefore the sage embraces the one.
Because he doesn't display himself,
people can see his light.
Because he has nothing to prove,
people can trust his words.
Because he doesn't know who he is,
people recognize themselves in him.
Because he has no goal in mind,
everything he does succeeds.
The old saying that the flexible are preserved
unbroken is surely right!
If you have attained wholeness,

everything will flock to you.

The flexible are preserved unbroken.
The bent become straight.
The empty are filled.
The exhausted become renewed.

A child in the womb occupies minimum space so that it gives its mother the least trouble as far as space is concerned. If it spreads its legs and hands, she will be put to great harm. She will not be able to accommodate the baby properly. This is 'law of minimum accommodation' as understood by me.

Prayers are done with great humility for we bend our heads. Some go down on their knees: some lie flat on the ground diminishing their heights to the maximum extent possible.

Flexibility of some trees is amazing. When strong winds blow, they sway to and fro. When the wind stops, they are back in their original form. This is the reason why they survive storms. Rigidity is death. Have we not seen dead person's body becoming rigid like a log of wood with the passing of time? Flexibility is life...rigidity is death...

Flexibility means the understanding which accepts 'I have my views...so do you! Everybody is entitled to what they perceive as correct as a political party, society or religion. Killing people of other religions seems to be a sacred duty to some. It is their understanding. Beyond religion is the 'mighty power' which is there, is and will be through eternity. Coming out of rigid religious belief will give relief to millions of people.

What is 'empty' referred to above? To my understanding it is not carrying any baggage of I, me and mine. Being empty is all inclusive ...all expansive...and like the sky, all pervading. Because it is all pervading, everything is made available.

Lao Tzu says: The rich are confounded.

The 'rich' wonder why the money they have amassed with such great labour is not giving them true and lasting joy, which they sought and thought that it could be bought with their money.

> **Therefore the sage embraces the one.**
> **Because he doesn't display himself,**
> **people can see his light.**
> **Because he has nothing to prove,**
> **people can trust his words.**
> **Because he doesn't know who he is,**
> **people recognize themselves in him.**
> **Because he has no goal in mind,**
> **everything he does succeeds.**
> **The old saying that the flexible are preserved**
> **unbroken is surely right!**
> **If you have attained wholeness,**
> **everything will flock to you.**

We all live in a highly competitive world. We want to achieve many things for which we have set ourselves some goals. These goals many times are time-bound. "Achieve this much in this much of time" is the mantra of many people wanting to prove themselves. This extreme competition leads to over-working and exhaustion. When a person over-works, either he goes on feasting junk food or goes on smoking or drinking soft-drinks, tea or coffee. There is no need for me to describe the results of such a life-style. The whole world seems to be caught in this trap called 'goals'.

A person who has attained wholeness (enlightened) is never worried about his future because of his total trust in his Mother. Without seeking, he is filled with everything. This, again, is another paradox in the life of a master.

23rd Verse

FUTILITY OF OVER EXERTION

To talk little is natural:
Fierce winds do not blow all morning;
a downpour of rain does not last the day.
Who does this? Heaven and earth.
But these are exaggerated, forced effects,
and that is why they cannot be sustained.
If heaven and earth cannot sustain a forced action,
how much less is man able to do?
Those who follow the Way
become one with the Way.
Those who follow goodness
become one with goodness.
Those who stray from the Way and goodness
become one with failure.
If you conform to the Way,
its power flows through you.
Your actions become those of nature,
your ways those of heaven.
Open yourself to the Tao

and trust your natural responses...
then everything will fall into place.

Power of speech and expression is the greatest gift we all have. Swami Vivekananda won over the people of the west and in due course the rest of the world, because of his power of speech. Politicians also use the power of their speech to bring people to their party. The speaker and the listener both know that behind the flowery speech lies the unabashed selfishness. Only a handful of people in politics want to truly serve the country: the rest of them use (or misuse) their power of speech.

Speeches that come from the soul for the betterment of people, take the form of books vcds or cds and become a guide for future generations. The speeches of politicians seldom come in printed form. In fact, their recorded speeches come as a matter of reference in the hands of their opponent as a tool to dethrone him. Mudslinging is the result of such false promises made by the power of oratory.

The politicians with their grimaces and facial gestures trying desperately to bring to notice whatever they want to say, is truly comical. They sway their hands, thump the tables, hold on to the mikes, look left and right to impress upon the audience. Oh, what a waste of energy! We have plenty of such jokers in politics. We can be grateful to them for they do entertain us free of cost!

Such speeches can be compared to storms: stirring up many things but achieving nothing but destruction and bringing sadness. They will not last long.

Going in silence or 'moun vrath' is observed by many spiritual people. Mahatma Gandhi also used to observe silence once a week. He was a great combination of a yogi and a stateman.

Not just saintly people, we can also experience the silence with which scientists work. They do not want to be disturbed. To achieve in any field, some sort of seclusion is needed.... minimum words creates maximum energy. Meditation naturally happens when we observe silence.

Another problem with speech is that words can be misquoted, misunderstood and misrepresented. Silence saves you from these calamities. All the scriptures are words meant to take you beyond, in silence. Beyond that is the silence ultimate!...the source of everything.

Impermanence is the quality of life. Neither happiness is permanent, nor unhappiness. Why seek happiness when that will also fade away after some time for which you have put in so much effort? Why be disturbed by the unpleasant happening because that is also temporary? He is wise who is able to see the futility of exaggerated, forced actions.

We have seen hot tempered persons blowing their top at the drop of a hat. Anger is the outcome of strong sense of ego which screams 'I am the best'. It seems to be their natural behavior. Has he been like that as a child? No....He unfortunately has fallen into his own self-created 'larger than life' image of himself and is squeezed from all sides. He can only scream and shout, as the grip of his ego is too tight.

When we surrender to Tao (God), and do our duties without forgetting the Great Force which works through every blade of grass, we are on our joyous journey back Home.

Bhagvad Gita: 18.65.

Occupy thy mind with Me, be devoted to Me, sacrifice to Me, bow down to Me. Thou shalt reach Myself; truly do I promise unto thee (for) thou art dear to Me.

24th Verse

DO AWAY WITH DISPLAYING

If you stand on tiptoe, you cannot stand firmly.
If you take long steps, you cannot walk far.
Showing off does not reveal enlightenment
Boasting will not produce accomplishment.
He who is self-righteous is not respected.
He who brags will not endure.
All these ways of acting are odious, distasteful.
They are superfluous excesses.
They are like pain in the stomach,
a tumor in the belly.
When walking the path of Tao,
this is the very stuff that must be
uprooted, thrown out, and left behind.

Masters use cryptic language. I surrender to this master's wisdom and guidance which sweeps me over and encourages me to venture into the depths of his verses. It is nothing but his grace that makes me to write a few lines on his profound wisdom.

Standing on a tip-toe is ego-based effort which claims ownership of every achievement. But, any failure, the very same person will have many reasons to blame like others, circumstances etc. It is like "heads I win ...tail you lose". Let us balance ourselves with both the legs...our effort and His Grace as our two legs. Without effort, there is no Grace... and without Grace, there can be no action. Like the eternal dispute about which came first, the egg or the chicken.... I have no answer..

Taking long steps tires out a person in a short time. Let us remember 'slow and steady wins the race'. Let us not hasten any activity. Let us do whatever we choose to do, in a more calm and collected way.

Even in day to day life, we shun people who brag and boast about their achievements. When we try to enter God's kingdom, our ego will retard our progress for it is like a heavy weight which will drag us down and drown us in untold misery. Lao Tzu is warning us about this baggage which can take any form...even that of a tumor in the stomach. Whether we become enlightened or not, let us atleast live in good health till our last breath. He compares ego to tumor and indirectly suggests that we come out of our ego trip.

Spiritual healers say that our emotions are stored in our stomach. It may be true, because we can see how people either over-eat or deny food when they are emotionally disturbed. We know that both can create physical problems.

Unconsciously and unwittingly we become victims of self-aggrandizement. A simpler way to come out of ego trip is to talk less and go in silence at least for an hour everyday. Another effective way is to go on a picnic without anybody. Being with nature, talking to the trees and chasing the butterflies will give you immense joy. This is another type of active meditation. This is my favourite meditation.

If bragging is ego in all its glory, there are other shades to it, like being self-righteous. "My way is the highway...and no other way." This attitude exists in every walk of our life and that includes spiritual organizations as well. I have been associated with many spiritual organizations and gurus, and I came out more confused about the simple three letter word "EGO." Nevertheless, I am grateful to them for propelling me towards God. Freedom is the essence of spirit.

"Casting away ego will shower us with ever-lasting joy and peace."

25th verse

THE SUPREME POWER

There was something formless and perfect
before the universe was born.
It is serene. Empty.
Solitary. Unchanging.
Infinite. Eternally present.
It is the Mother of the universe.
For lack of a better name I call it Tao.
I call it great.
Great is boundless;
boundless is eternally flowing;
ever flowing, it is constantly returning.
Therefore, the Way is great,
heaven is great,
earth is great,
people are great.

Thus, to know humanity,
understand the earth.
To know earth,

understand heaven.
To know heaven,
understand the Way.
To know the Way,
understand the great within yourself.

Lao Tzu says that formless is perfect. All adjectives that we use are for the forms. Any energy is formless; be it electrical or magnetic or whatever and as such they are perfect, just perfect. When does it become imperfect? It becomes imperfect when it is used by us for various reasons. For its use can also be misused. There is no need to elaborate on this aspect of use and misuse.

Again, any 'form' has its limitations in its functioning. We cannot run like cheetah...we cannot jump from branch to branch like a monkey...we cannot hang upside down like a bat. In fact, no human can be like another person. These defects are because of forms. Lao Tzu is talking about the Supreme Power or Eternal God that has no particular form. This makes Him become every form that is seen and unseen.

How did all the million trillion galaxies came into existence? And out of What? This is a common question to a scientist as well as a spiritual aspirant. Scientists start analyzing the material things. When we have this vastness called universe, where is he going to start from? may be under a microscope. Spirituality makes no external effort probing for an answer for, through meditation, the enlightened person understands the origin of the universe. Behind all the visible forms we call universe, is the eternal silence.. serenity...simplicity...the origin of everything. As everything has emerged from This, It must be the mother. Lao Tzu prefers to calls it Tao, 'THE GREAT'.

Physically, all of us are endowed with 5 sense organs and 5 organs of cognition. The only difference between an enlightened person and the others is that they have put in efforts to know and understand life beyond the experiences enjoyed (suffered) by the body.

Lao Tzu repeats the word 'great...great...great' that existed before creation and will exist throughout eternity. Here I remember one story from the Indian epic Mahabharata. The story is like this. Yudhistira the eldest of the Pandavas, an embodiment of all virtues was asked to find atleast one person who was not good. He returned looking unhappy for he could not find even one. Duryodana, the eldest of the 100 Kaurava brothers who were evil incarnate was asked to find at least one good person. He also returns with a sad face saying that not even one good person could be found.

The Master Lao Tzu is like the Yudhistira. He finds only 'greatness' everywhere.

Take time to observe a tiny little ant. It contains brain, reproductive system, digestive system and every other thing all rolled into the tiny little body. Not just visible forms like ants..even the invisible microbes and viruses make the scientific community run for some solution from these monsters' attack. Are they not great that such intellectuals being like the scientists are chasing them them for whatever reasons?

Similarly a criminal also makes people search for him. The police, the forensic department, the law enforcing authorities and also the general public seem to take interest in him! In fact, one criminal gives job opportunity to hundreds of people. Similarly, one sick man gives job to many people to serve him. Some are visible like the doctors nurses etc. The invisible list cannot be measured. There are chemists, their assistants, the people involved in their transportation....endless seems to be the list.

Gurus are like the sign-board. 'This way to God'. Beyond that, it is our own journey where nobody is needed or has any place.

In the previous chapters, ego was lambasted. In this verse, Lao Tzu is asking us to understand our own greatness. The ideas expressed look contradictory.

Who is great and what is greatness?

Achievement in life is considered to be great by many of us. A person standing first in the university exam becomes 'great achiever'. What was his achievement? All the knowledge that he gathered while studying for his exams were rooted in his memory and he used this memory to his advantage. Hence his memory is 'great'. Another student forgets what he has studied. He had great loss of memory ! Hence loss of memory is equally great! A difficult concept indeed! Let us ponder over it.

What is the difference between 'ego' of a person and the enlightened master's experience which says "I am great"?

Ego screams 'I am the best'. Enlightenment whispers; 'I am great...but so are you...and so is everything seen and unseen.'

When we get this vision of Greatness, we suffer no more. Fear of death does not grip us any more for we understand that everything comes and goes. The inter-connectivity, the inner connectivity and inter-dependence is experienced by everybody but not appreciated by anybody.

No wonder Lao Tzu says: Tao is Great!...Tao is Great.!.. Tao is Great!..

People who understand his message say: Lao Tzu is great!...Lao Tzu is great !..Lao Tzu is great!

Bhagvad Gita: 7.7. Beyond Me, O Dhananjaya(Arjuna) there is naught. All this is strung in Me, as a row of jewel on a thread.

26th Verse

SERENITY IS SAINTLY

The heavy is the root of light.
The still is the master of unrest.
Realizing this,
the successful person is
poised and centered
in the midst of all activities;
although surrounded by opulence,
he is not swayed.
Why should the lord of the country
flit about like a fool?
If you let yourself be blown to and fro,
you lose touch with your root.
To be restless is to lose one's self- mastery.

"Heavy" is not about the weight. Heavy, to my understanding means that which is immovable...that which is immovable is always there, all the time. It can be compared to the invisible foundation of a visible structure.

The foundation has to be strong for the whole building is dependent on it. To put it simply, the structure depends on the foundation.

Another comparison we have is the ocean and the waves. The waves constantly rise and fall...appear and disappear. But deep down is the sea...still and silent.....ever present ... and is always the cause for the waves to exist.

A master is like the ocean. Still and deep and yet he becomes the cause of many activities performed for the betterment of people and the environment. He is not perturbed about the things that happen around him while he relentlessly works for the society. Bouquets and brickbats are received with equanimity. One who can transcend beyond likes and dislikes good and bad can never be disturbed by anything outside of him for he is established in his own self which is too powerful to be shaken.

When we work in an office, school or college or anywhere for that matter, we get paid. Can we even imagine how much a master must be getting when he works for the whole world? It is not just about money. The greatest gift that he receives is the good-will which can never be measured in terms of money.

Seek first the kingdom of God...said Jesus. How to seek the kingdom? Where is it? How to reach there? The whole cosmos is God's kingdom. Before thinking about the cosmos, let us start with the earth where we live. Let us embrace all of it, the whole of it and work for it. Such work will be possible only if there is unselfish love. Thus, unselfish love is the foundation on which our activity should be based upon.

This Love is Tao...the Great!.

27th Verse

MASTER IS A MYSTERY

A knower of the truth
travels without leaving a trace,
speaks without causing harm,
gives without keeping an account.
The door he shuts, though having no lock,
cannot be opened.
The knot he ties, though using no cord,
cannot be undone.

Be wise and help all being impartially,
abandoning none.
Waste no opportunities.
This is called following the light.

What is a good man but a bad man's teacher?
What is a bad man but a good man's job?
If the teacher is not respected
and the student is not cared for

**confusion will arise, however clever one is.
This is a great secret.**

The world we all live now is very insecure. There is fear everywhere and this prevents us from helping our next door neighbor. Richer a person gets, more is the insecurity he experiences. His privacy is lost, as all the time he is surrounded by people to protect him. The protection they give is not out of love for that person, but for the love of money that they will be getting. If somebody pays more than this person, they will jump over the fence. There is no loyalty when money is the only consideration for looking after somebody.

In my childhood, I have read stories about some hidden wealth which is guarded by poisonous snakes which will not allow any body to go near it. Neither the snake is benefitted nor can anybody claim it. Then comes a brave Prince to charm the snake, kill it and claim the booty.

A true master comes as the brave prince described above. He leads us to true treasure killing the snake called ego.

When film stars or politicians come to visit some place, the other people of that city have to go through lot of inconveniences. There was an incident reported about the unfortunate death of a patient, as the vehicle could not reach the hospital on time because a VIP was on his way. Such travels of these VIPs cause so much inconvenience.

When we live in trust with each other, we neither need doors nor locks. Shani-Shinganapur, a small town in Maharashtra, is a strange place in this world. There are no doors in any of the houses in this place. The belief behind this is that the presiding devata (God) Shani will harm whoever lays his hands on others property where He resides.

A small, soft, weapon a few inches long, can cause more harm than any atom bombs:. ....our tongues. People spit venom and incite people and usurp them to destruction. Hate-speech is supported by hate-mails and within a few minutes, thousands of people take up arms to destroy others. This is misuse of our capabilities and our technology. Can hate be cured by hate? I do not think so....These misguided persons need more compassion and love than others. The invisible cord or connection is love. If all of us take a vow and send unconditional love to these people, I am sure we can experience heaven on earth.

I remember a Hindi movie, "Do ankhein barah haath". The literal meaning is two eyes and 12 hands....one jailor and 6 criminals. The jailor tries to reform the 6 condemned criminals, wins over them and transforms them by his love and compassion.

India has a very great tradition of reverence to their gurus. We have 'guru poornima' celebrations where we show our love and gratitude to our teachers. Teachers, even at mundane level, are needed for us to learn. You may think that we can also learn from books or internet but a knowledgeable and authentic person is needed to clarify our doubts.

Gurus guide us on our spiritual path showing us the way to live in peace and harmony. Many of the gurus are surrounded by unscrupulous persons and I used to wonder, even doubt, about the integrity of my guru. But now, after almost 30 years of being in spirituality, I understand that gurus never abandon anybody. If he abandons, he can never be a guru. He could have abandoned me too. Though not a criminal in the ordinary sense, I had a lot of negativity deep down within me. I take this opportunity to thank him from the bottom of my heart for leading me gently, silently, into Light.

Bhagvad Gita: 6.9. He attains excellence who looks with equal regard upon well-wishers, friends, foes, neutrals, arbiters, the hateful, the relatives, and upon the righteous and the unrighteous alike.

28th Verse

BE A GARDENER

Know the strength of man,
but keep a woman's care!
Be a valley under heaven;
if you do, the constant virtue
will not fade away.
One will become like a child again.

Know the white,
keep the black,
and be the pattern of the world.
to move constantly in the path of virtue
without erring a single step,
and to return again to the infinite.

One who understands splendor
while holding to humility
acts in accord with eternal power.
To be the fountain of the world is
to live the abundant life of virtue.

**When the unformed is formed into objects,
its original qualities are lost.
If you preserve your original qualities,
you can govern anything.
Truly, the best governor governs least.**

'Know the Masculine'... Masculine is a symbolic expression for aggressiveness, power, authority, control etc. A ruler, who, in spite of being in power and position, remains gentle and soft while dealing with his subjects, will naturally be loved and cared for.

Lao Tzu is also asking us to awaken the tenderness in our hearts. It symbolizes the feminine aspect of us. Shankaracharya says; 'kuputraha jayathe kadachit, kumata na bhavati' which means: ...there can be a bad son, but never a bad mother. Indian tradition says, matru devo bhava 'mother is God'...the father comes next, guru is given third place and the guests, the fourth.

Hinduism symbolically expresses this idea of a balance between authority (masculine) and amity(feminine) in the form of Ardhanareeshwar...half-man...half woman.

Lao Tzu asks us to be like a valley which receives all the water that pours down as rain. It also welcomes all the boulders, rocks, pebbles, broken branches, dried up leave... in fact, everything that is discarded by the mountains. It does not choose between good and bad. The valley receives everything with graceful equanimity.

Be like a child, he says. Child has no preferences. It can play with the rich or poor...high caste or low caste...It does not differentiate for it has not yet developed ego which is like the iron wall.

People have different qualities at different times. Their colours change from white to black and all shades of grey in between. A ruler who is immersed in the divine, will be able to create the most beautiful pattern with these people because he know how to handle them... strict, yet gentle.

"Understand splendor" says the master. To understand something, one must have the experience. Experiences can never be borrowed. Living a virtuous life opens the door to all glory...all splendors....all grandeur. In spite of all his chievements, he remains humble and modest.

What is our 'original quality'?. According to Hinduism, we are Prema Swaroopa (embodiment of love) ...Ananda Swaroopa...(embodiment of bliss). That was our original state. How did we degrade ourselves? Because of our ego, we have fallen down into such an abysmal position. Ego knows only to boss over...to control and command by fair means or foul. How can such person receive any love or respect?

A true ruler is the one who is an embodiment of virtue. Yatha raja..tatha praja..says a Sanskrit adage which means; as the king, so are the people. If people in power and position think over these words of wisdom from the great master Lao Tzu, heaven is right here and now itself!

Bhagvad Gita: verse 3.21 whatever the superior person does, that is followed by others. What he demonstrates by action, that people follow.

29th Verse

LIVING IN BALANCE

Do you think you can take over the universe and improve it?
I do not believe it can be done.

Everything under heaven is a sacred vessel and cannot be controlled.
Trying to control leads to ruin.
Trying to grasp, we lose.

Allow your life to unfurl naturally.
Know that it too is a vessel of perfection.
Just as you breathe in and breathe out,
there is a time for being ahead
and a time for being behind;
a time for being in motion
and a time for being at rest;
a time for being vigorous
and a time for being exhausted;
a time for being safe

and a time for being in danger.
To the sage
all of life is movement towards perfection,
so what need has he
for the excessive, the extravagant or the extreme?

Hindu rituals are incomplete without cocoanut. Many times, they are smeared with either turmeric powder or sandalwood powder and tilak (red vermilion powder) is applied.

There is a story behind this coconut.

A folk lore says that Sage Vishvamitra held a pole to arrest the fall of Trishanku from heaven. The pole became the cocoanut tree, and Trishanku's head became the cocoanut. The fiber of cocoanut became the beard and when you take it off, you see his eyes peering at you.

Power of penance of Vishvamitra turns an ordinary pole into a tree. This is also sort of creation in a humble way. We cannot create a cocoanut tree but can make an offering of it to the Great Creator thus offering ourselves in all humility. The cocoanut has three eyes and humans posses two physical eyes and the third eye that lies in between the eyes brows opens itself as we progress in our spiritual path. Thus we can also see that a cocoanut almost resembles a human head. This is one of the explanations as to why cocoanuts are offered during religious ceremonies by Hindus.

All the scientists in the world are making futile attempts to create artificial body parts. While their hard work and dedication is laudable, they can never replicate God's creation. Let us preserve the creation. It exists in such abundance that there is no need to add or subtract even a blade of grass to it. Look after grass that grows at the back-yard. It has its place in creation. Looking after one's own health by having regular exercise, balanced food taken on time and silence (meditation) of 15 to 20 minutes per day will take care of health to a great extent. We thus do our best to the best of His creation, that is you and me! And let us continue to keep our virtues and high ideals.

Lao Tzu compares creation to a vessel. This vessel contains all the 10,000 things that we have been discussing about right from the first chapter onwards. The vessel or the container has to be bigger than the contents to hold them properly. The simple understanding is that the Creator is bigger than creation.

The world has woken up to the health hazards due to extensive use of insecticides and pesticides. The scientists are alarmed at the resistance power of so many types of viruses and microbes that affect not just humans, but also animals and birds. The best way to escape from them is to go back to nature where solutions to all problems of life are hidden in the roots, barks, leaves, fruits and flowers. Neem tree is world famous for its anti-bacterial properties.

"Trying to control lead to ruin", the master says. ...Cutting down trees indiscriminately for our monetary gains has become the main cause of many animals and birds facing extinction. Those who survive leave their original habitat and move inwards to human settlements in search of food and water. Instead of taking positive steps towards such migration, many of them are poisoned by the local people.

Snakes are killed in thousands many times out of ignorance which is based on fear. Rodents which destroy crops are the main food of the snakes thus saving the crops from destruction. To control rodents, pesticides and dangerous chemicals are used which are absorbed by the plants and crops. You and I are the indirect victims of artificially trying to control snakes, rodents and pests.

Death happens when we stop breathing. Nobody wants to die ...then why did breathing stop for the person who never wants to die? We have no answers to such questions. We breathe in and also breathe out. Both are needed. We need to work...we need rest...we need day as much as we need night...we need the sun to warm us and the moon to soothe us. To appreciate our own health, we need ill-health! The whole world exists in pairs of opposites. There is no way anybody can do anything about it. The wisdom is to go with the flow while doing our best in our chosen field of activity.

Before electricity was invented, people withdrew themselves from activity till the next day. With artificial lights, we have no nights....no rest...no peace! In fact, it is considered fashionable to have mid-night parties and come home in the morning and sleep till the evening. We are going against nature and creating disharmony. If we can align ourselves at least to some extent with the rising and setting sun, we can enjoy better physical, emotional and mental health.

Let the verses be not understood as a passive acceptance which will lead to lethargy. In fact, when Krishna is asking the reluctant Arjuna to fight, the Lord also says: "I have nothing to achieve...nothing is there which is not Mine..still I continue to act"...This is a message for people who cover themselves with a blanket called inaction, born out of fear of failures and philosophizing things and saying 'It is God's will". If everything is God's will, do not eat or drink! Can we remain like that more than a few days?

Discriminating quality is unique to humans only. Discrimination is the off-spring of living in balance... balance is a divine quality which is inherent in all of us.

Let us awaken ourselves to our own divinity.

30th Verse

PROTECT- DO NOT PLUNDER

One who would guide a leader of men in the uses
of life
will warn him against the use of arms of conquest.
Weapons often turn upon the wielder.

Where armies settle,
nature offers nothing but briars and thorns.
After a great battle has been fought,
the land is cursed, the crops fail,
the earth lies stripped of its motherhood.

After you have attained your purpose,
you must not parade your success,
you must not boast of your ability,
you must not feel proud;
you must rather regret that you had not been
able to prevent the war.

You must never think of conquering others by force.
Whatever strains with force
will soon decay.
It is not attuned to the Way.
Not being attuned to the Way,
its end comes all too soon.

What does "uses of life" mean? Life means growth, continuation, prolongation, maintenance, protection, and also many other qualities where perpetuation is signified.

A ruler gives 'life' means he is responsible for the safety of his subjects.

In India, in good old days, the king used to have a Rishi or holy man as his Guru. The king used to consult his Guru in matter of not only spirituality and religion, but wise governance and administration also. Chanakya was a good example of a Guru capable of guiding the king Chandragupta Maurya. There are innumerable such examples in our Indian history.

A person who guides a king is called a 'mantri' or minister. As Indians, we know that a mantra means a holy sound or verse. The word mantri must have been a derivative of the word mantra. That means his words are to be followed. His duty is to guide the king and in turn his subjects towards prosperity and peace. He is supposed to be a wise man who the king respects and reveres and listens to. The minister's counsel and guidance as to how to run a country, budgeting of finances etc. make him a living treasure. It is also his duty to keep a vigilant eye on the king who appointed him. If he feels the king is going astray, he becomes his anchor and advisor. A king should use his army only to defend and not to offend.

We try to prolong the life of our lifeless (inanimate object) vehicles and gadgets by taking proper care either by servicing it ourselves or taking the help of somebody who is good at repairing and maintaining things. This is how we prolong the lives of non-living things.

If non-living things are given so much importance, how much care should a ruler take of his living subjects!

"weapons often turn upon the wielder"

Jesus says "one who rules by the sword shall die by it". Unfortunately, Jesus' words are forgotten and Jesus remains as a statue or a holy cross for us to worship. If His words are forgotten and not followed, our worship is meaningless. The resurrection of Jesus, the Christ, will happen again if we follow His teachings in all earnest.

Plants need water to grow and not blood of those who get killed and the salty tears of those who are left behind. Lao Tzu says only thorns and thistles will grow where there is bloodshed. He warns us that such land will be cursed. When people are killed in thousands in a war, prosperity and peace are buried with the people.

We still have time. We can go to such areas where people constantly live in fear and share their grief. If that is not possible, form groups of peace loving people and pray that good sense prevails. We have such beautiful group in Pune called soul circle. When we shed tears in repentance and take a pledge to reform ourselves, even the salty water that flows from our eyes will have the power to bring forth life in a barren land.

**After you have attained your purpose,
you must not parade your success,
you must not boast of your ability,
you must not feel proud;
you must rather regret that you had not been
able to prevent the war.**

Does winning a war bring happiness?

The Pandavas won the Mahabharata war but lost all their children. In spite of such great personal tragedy, the duty-bound Pandavas ruled their country for some years and then finally left for the Himalayas seeking the Great Peace. The Pandavas regretted that they could not prevent the war as the atrocity of Kauravas was beyond tolerance.

It will take too much of space to narrate fully the Mahabharata war and the circumstances under which the Pandavas entered the battle field with great reluctance. Even before entering the battle field, Arjuna could foresee the deadly aftermath of the war and pleaded for avoiding the war.

Suffice it to say, in a war, nobody wins. Both the parties lose their people and their animals and become an instrument in creating war widows, fatherless children and helpless old parents.

Spreading the message of peace will gently massage and heal the wounded hearts and bring back life into the lives of broken people afflicted in different ways due to war. Let us join hands in this holy task. Such messengers will become massagers of the world we live in. Love is the only salve the world needs now. Otherwise we shall live as 'slaves' ...just re-arranging the spelling gives insight as to what is needed to be done.

Person like Buddha conquered the world by love and compassion and not by waging war. Instead of just worshipping His image, let us follow his teaching to the best of our ability. Then only we can call ourselves followers or devotees of Lord Budhha.

Bhagvad Gita: verse 9.22. (part of it).... I carry what they lack and preserve what they already have.

———◆◈◆———

31st Verse

WEANING FROM WEAPONS

Fine weapons of war augur evil.
Even things seem to hate them.
Therefore a man of Tao does not set his heart upon them.

In ordinary life, a gentleman regards the left side as the place of honour:
In war, the right side is the place of honour.

As weapons are instruments of evil,
they are not properly a gentleman's instruments;
Only on necessity will he resort to them.
For peace and quiet are dearest to his heart,
and to him even a victory is no cause for rejoicing.
To rejoice over a victory, is to rejoice over the slaughter of men!
Hence a man who rejoices over the slaughter of men cannot expect to thrive in the world of men.
On happy occasion the left side is preferred:

On sad occasion the right side.
In the army the Lieutenant Commander stands on the left,
while the Commander- in -Chief stands on the right.
This means that war is treated on par with funeral service.

Because many people have been killed,
it is only right that the survivors should mourn for them.
Hence, even a victory is a funeral..

According to Lao Tzu, weapons are instruments of evil. They are to be used only for self protection and not destruction. He says "even things hate them". Scientists have proved that trees and plants respond to our emotions. Lao Tzu goes one step further and says that even things (non-living things) hate them. That is his sensitivity.

The first chapter of Bhagvad Gita is called : "Vishada Yog': (meaning : yoga of grief.)

In this chapter(starting from verse number 28 to 46) Arjuna describes to Lord Krishna his physical and mental conditions that are terribly affected by even the thought of war. Instead of quoting the many verses, let me just give the gist of this chapter. The distraught Arjuna laments his fate which has dragged him into waging war with his own cousin brothers, gurus and respected elders of his family. He tried his level best to avoid war because he knew the outcome of even so-called victory would have its foundations on dead bodies of people.

He says he would prefer death than to kill his own kith and kin. He is scared about the aftermath of such wars and is worried about the condition of the females, the war widows, and young fatherless children that are left behind when the male members are killed in the war.

Arjuna further says that even if all the three worlds are offered to him as gift of victory, still he desires them not... that being his attitude towards the impending war, what to say of some kingdom! (for which they are waging war). For Arjuna, peaceful living outweighs all the riches one can think of.

Lao Tzu says "war is treated on par with funeral".

Whoever enters a war, knows very well that he can also be killed before he kills his enemies. He has dug his own untimely grave. While leading his army, he is leading them to death and thus becomes a 'leader of death'.

War is not about just killing of humans. In these days of high tech machines crores of rupees are spent. Such huge money could have been used to save lives. In fact these factories are making coffins for thousands of lives. Our brain power is used for destroying lives. Wars create only graveyards.

Graveyards of soldiers killed in war silently give us the message of futility of wars.

32nd Verse

HEAVEN ON EARTH

Tao is always nameless.
Small as it is in its Primal Simplicity,
It is inferior to nothing in the world.
If only a ruler could cling to it,
everything will render homage to him.
Heaven and Earth will be harmonized and send
down sweet dew.
Peace and order will reign among the people without
any command from above.

When once the Primal Simplicity diversified,
Different names appeared.
Are there not enough names now?

Is this not the time to stop?
To know when to stop is to preserve ourselves from
danger.

The Tao is the world what a great river or an ocean is to the streams and brooks.

The master refers to the Supreme power which we call God "as simple and nameless." The opening chapter itself has this message of "One Supreme Power"; to explain again will be a repetition, which I would like to avoid.

Worshiping this Supreme Power in different ways has lead to having many places of worship and thus confining this all pervasive power into small little places called temples, churches, synagogues, mosques etc. The major religions unfortunately are also sub divided and each sub division is at war with its other sects, its own people.

Lord Krishna was born in Yadava Dynasty. Because of some unfortunate incidents, the people of that clan fought amongst themselves and killed their own people.

In fact, the whole world seems to be fighting only for God but say that God is Love and Peace! May we develop peace on our hearts and let people enjoy connecting to this supreme power in the way they want to.

Lao Tzu uses the 'opposite' to explain a concept. Paradox is his way of explaining the inexplicable. He says - it is inferior to nothing ...means it is superior to everything!

Whenever we ask for favours, we give more value to object of our desire and this naturally means God is less important. It is truly unfortunate that He becomes important as much as He fulfills my desires.

If the king rules his kingdom with the awareness of the 'all powerful' and holds on to the "Truth"(that everything is like pearls strung on a thread), that would truly be the heaven on earth we all dream about! Because of his understanding that behind the all the manifested things is the unmanifested "Great One"(Supreme power) he rules his kingdom without using authority or power. People co-operate and coexist peacefully for there is no fear coming down on them from the rulers in the form of rules and regulations.

The 'Primal Simplicity', this Supreme Power, in due course was misrepresented by the so-called religious leaders. They used fear as the main weapon to subjugate people. Even a ten-digit number when divided by the smallest denominator 2 will become smaller and smaller when it is further and further divided. This division is called religion. There are other divisions as well based on caste, colour, language etc. We have all forgotten our glory of being a part of God and have become apart..torn apart...in such a way that it is going to be a uphill task to unite people of the world.

In Lao Tzu's style of explaining in paradoxes, let us hope and pray that if religion can divide, it can also unite!

The master is asking a straight question:

'Are they not enough names now'?

Let no body start a new religion or a new cult. We have had enough...more than enough, of religions.

The world does not need any new religion now.

Or maybe we do need a new religion; this new religion will be nameless like Tao and it can be called as Universal Love!

Bhagvad Gita: verse 12.3 and 12.4.(combined)

But those also, who worship the Imperishable, the Indefinable, the Unmanifested, the Omnipresent, the

Unthinkable, the Unchangeable, the Immovable, the Eternal – having subdued all the senses, even-minded everywhere, engaged in the welfare of all being – verily, they reach only Myself.

33rd Verse

SELF-VICTORY

**He who knows men is clever;
he who knows himself has insight.
He who conquers men has force;
he who conquers himself is truly strong.
He who knows when he has got enough is rich,
and he who adheres assiduously to the path of Tao
is a man of steady purpose.
He who stays where he has found his true home
endures long,
and he who dies but perishes not enjoys real longevity.**

In the mundane world, to survive one has to know about the people he is dealing with. Smartness is needed to survive in this world.

How does a saint survive in such a world? He survives because he has conquered himself (self-realized soul). A saintly person does not use his physical power or power of speech to attract others. In fact, Lord Buddha remained silent for many years. People from far and wide came to him to find meaning of life.

Illusion is called as 'maya' in Sanskrit and other languages in India. A man walking in the desert encounters 'maya' many times. The shining sand appears to be water. A man of illusion feels money is the only thing in life. Because of such wrong understanding nothing seems to be enough for him. His whole life is about amassing wealth and in that hot pursuit he burns himself out. There is a saying in Sanskrit "nitya tripthaha te nitya mukthaha"...one who is satisfied (with whatever he has) is a liberated soul.

When our 'ego' dies, we are born again...just like a new born, our nature becomes pure and perfect.

Anything born has to die someday.

What then is immortality or eternal life as some holy books describe?

Immortality or deathlessness is achieved when we discard our ego and surrender to the Supreme power working in mysterious ways for millions of years, while playing our allotted roles on this earth.

Bhagvad Gita: verse 13.27.

He sees, who sees the Supreme Lord, exiting equally in all being, deathless in the dying.

34th Verse

THE SOURCE OF EVERYTHING

The Great Tao is universal like a flood.
How can it be turned to the right or to the left?
All creatures depend on it,
and it denies nothing to anyone.
It does its work,
but it makes no claim for itself.
It clothes and feeds all,
but it does not lord it over them:
Thus it may be called "the Little".

All things return to it as to their home,
but it does not lord it over them:
Thus, it may be called "the Great".

It is just because it does not wish to be great
that its greatness is fully realized.

Water is precious to every living thing. Civilization developed mainly along rivers. As a school girl I have read that "Egypt is the gift of Nile".

Every living being depends on water directly or indirectly for sustenance. We depend on water. What does water depend on?

It depends on Tao.

We are all the consumers....the Producer is Tao.

Before electricity was invented, agriculture flourished mainly along river banks. Rivers also helped the farmers in transporting their products.

A saint-poet says: "nadia na piye kabhi apna jal...vruksh na khaye kabhi apna phal." which means the river does not drink its own water...nor does a tree eat its own fruit..

The creation is for the consumers...you and me...

Even the most solid looking food has water hidden in it.

Whether we have gratitude and reverence or not, water does its duty to all the creation.

Whether we acknowledge and revere the Creator (Tao) or not, its Power is over-whelming and ever flowing.

We have to some extent, power over water which takes the shape of dams, bunds etc. But when a tidal wave breaks, what can we do?

Who can stop the tsunami?

Who is capable of directing its course?

We have a tendency to keep some people on a high pedestal because of their contribution to the society, country or the world at large. We label some people 'great' for their contribution in their chosen field of action...be it in the world of music, fine arts, politics, social and spiritual revolutions, science and technology and so on.

Such people do affect humanity in a positive way. There have been revolutionaries who have brought about tremendous change in the way we think and act.

But, whether one comes under this category of 'great' or not, we consume water. So far, no body has given a title to the all-sustaining power of water, nor has anybody given due credit to it. Fortunately, atleast a few cultures have recognized the greatness of this great power called "water". We in India worship river and oceans and river is worshipped as a female and the ocean as male.

Again we see the glimpses of message contained in Bhagavad Gita; do your duty...make no claim to its results...

Bhagvad Gita verse 15.13. Entering the earth with My energy I support all beings, and I nourish all the herbs, becoming the watery moon.(the watery moon: the Soma, moon, is considered as repository of all fluids.)

———◆◆◆———

35th Verse

LIFE OF A SAINT

He who holds the Great Symbol will attract all things to him.
They flock to him and receive no harm, for in him they find peace, security and happiness.
Music and dainty dishes can only make a passing guest pause.
But the words of Tao possess lasting effects,
though they are mild and flavorless,
though they appeal neither to the eye nor to the ear.

In ordinary life, we see people flocking around rich and famous people in the hope of receiving some favors from them.

When people with money and power attract others (for whatever reason) how much will a man who has surrendered to Tao attract? It is beyond words. All the power and prosperity of all the people put together will also be no match for the glory of Tao. In fact, every power and prosperity originates from Tao.

The so-called people with power many times resort to violence and other nefarious activities. They, many times, resort to 'contract killings' to get rid of their enemies. There is a constant struggle and this struggle to be at the top, topples them one day and they will be left with no place to hide and no people to comfort.

Contrary to this, is the joyous existence of a person of Tao. Such a person, seeks nothing, harms nobody and lives is such palpable peace that even a criminal feels safe with such a person.

Now let us discuss happiness.

What is happiness?

Different people will give different ideas and opinions as they perceive. Happiness for some is becoming famous...for some, it is accumulating wealth:for some it is power: eating good food and satisfying our five sense organs is also a way of finding happiness.

Over-indulgence in trying to satisfy our insatiable urge for variety leads to great suffering in due course. This is the plight of ordinary people.

One who has conquered himself, has no special likes or dislikes, is even minded in pain and pleasure and in loss and gain, is indeed close to Tao.

Even when he (the man of Tao) casts away his body, people build monuments or build samadhi (tomb) around his place of rest and visit the place for comfort and peace. As in life and so in death, such is the glory of a person of Tao!

Monuments are also built around famous personalities. People go there as visitors and not as devotees (there could be some exception).

Lao Tzu is making reference to symbols. We have symbols in every walk of our life. In arithmetic, it is +, -, etc. Water is H2O, oxygen is O. Hospitals and ambulances have a red + sign on them.

What symbol does Tao have?

Tao holds everything together.

We hold (embrace) people we love.

Tao holds all 'that is' ... 'that is' is His Greatest Love energy.

When we develop this sort of love for everything and everybody around us, we hold the symbol of Tao.

In the shadow of such great personality, even wild animals feel no animosity.

Bhagvad Gita 13.28.

Since seeing the Lord equally existent everywhere, he injures not Self by self, and so goes to the highest Goal.

(A self-realized person knows the Oneness behind the multitudes. He understands that whatever he does to other, he is the first person to receive it. If such wisdom has dawned on him, how can he ever hurt others?)

36th Verse

FAR FROM PUBLIC NOTICE

What is in the end to be shrunken,
begins by being first stretched out.
What is in the end to be weakened,
begins by being first made strong.
What is in the end to be thrown down,
begins by being first set on high.
What is in the end to be despoiled,
begins by being first richly endowed.

Herein is the subtle wisdom of life:
The soft and weak overcomes the hard and strong.
Just as the fish must not leave the deeps,
so the rulers must not display his weapons.

Lao Tzu, in his own inimitable style explains the dichotomous nature of things.

Animals meant to be slaughtered are well fed and taken good care so that they have no disease. Such care is given, not because of love for the animals, but for some ulterior motive.

To catch fish, a bait is thrown. The fish, lured by the bait, leaves its depth and gets hooked to the food (the bait) and is eventually killed. We also behave like the fish. The bait is in the form of money, various delicacies, attraction with the opposite sex etc.

The fish baited dies only once. But the intelligent being that we are, get trapped constantly by the world outside and die every day in some way till we finally bid good bye to this world.

Lao tzu's message is for the people in power. Weapons are symbols of power. Such display throws a challenge to the enemies. Time, talent, men and material are spent for inventing different new methods of mass destruction. If the world wakes up to the message of Lao Tzu, the same energies can take care of millions suffering without food and shelter.

Discretion and not display in the use of weapons is the need of the day.

People who try to spread their religion under threat are actually doing harm to their own faith. God does not need anybody to protect Him. Pray, who is protecting whom? I protect God or God protects me?

Let us think over it...

Real strength of a ruler is not displaying weapons of war.

There are different types of power. The two main power that are under discussion is money and speech. People with power of speech many times misuse this power. Unscrupulous politicians use their power of speech to attract gullible citizens. Promising great future and cheating people into believing their words is also misuse of power of speech.

Sugary words are used to lure innocent people into flesh trade falls in this category. As simple as a chocolate is given to small children to be misused by criminals -atrocity at its highest.

37ᵗʰ Verse

TO BRING HEAVEN ON EARTH

Tao never makes any ado,
and yet it does everything.
If a ruler can cling to it,
all things will grow of themselves.

When they have grown and tend to make a stir,
it is time to keep them in their place by the aid of the
nameless Primal Simplicity,

Which alone can curb the desires of men.
When the desires of men are curbed, there will be
peace,
and the world will settle down of its own accord.

How can a ruler (a man in power) rule his kingdom
effortlessly?

Lao Tzu says: "cling to it (Tao)".

Devotion and implicit faith in the Supreme Power which is running this cosmos is the only correct way to run a kingdom.

The whole world is in great restlessness because of strong difference of opinion about who should be worshipped and in what way. People are massacred in the name of God who is Mercy Personified.

To me, there are no atheists. When we admire the mighty ocean, enjoy the gentle breeze, feel awestruck at earthquakes, stand helpless in a blizzard...we are all unconsciously bowing down to this Mighty Power.

This Mighty power is available for all of us on this earth.

Let us use our resources with reverence and gratitude.

In India, no work is undertaken without bowing down to the Supreme Power. Even movie producers (the highly glamorous industry in India) start off their shooting with prayers. Public work like constructing dams, bridges, roads, etc.also follow this ritual of breaking a coconut before commencing their work.

In fact, every walk of life, from birth to death, the Supreme Power is invoked in India.

Hinduism has many rituals from pregnancy (baby shower) which is not just celebrating motherhood, but also invoking God to bless the yet-to-be-born child. Once it arrives, there are ceremonies regarding naming the child. Before entering formal school life, the children are initiated into 'Vidya Arambham" or initiation of knowledge.

As life is in cycles, again there comes a day when the child becomes an adult. The girl child attains puberty which again is celebrated. (this practice is much less now).

Marriage is a big event in any person's life. In the southern part of India, the boy ties a holy thread around the girl's neck (it is called as mangal sutra). India being a country with great variety, it will be out of place to write about the rituals in other parts of India. As I belong to south India, I shall confine myself to the rituals that are performed there.

As in life, so in death...There are rituals for the departed soul.

The painful parting that happens with death has many rituals, seeking blessings for the people they leave behind as Hinduism strongly believes in the theory of karma and re-incarnation of soul. Such rituals, especially for the departed soul, bring the family together forgetting all previous bitterness and enmity. If understood in the correct perspective, rituals are great binding factors.

In spite of such richness, why there is such hunger and disease in this country?

The answer is simple.

It is because of the human greed, indifference, or irresponsibility that many public undertakings remain incomplete or finished off haphazardly.

If everybody becomes conscious of their duties and responsibilities, we will create Heaven on Earth.

38ᵗʰ Verse

KNOWING THE DIFFERENCE

High Virtue is non-virtuous; therefore it has Virtue.
Low Virtue never frees itself from virtuousness;
therefore it has no Virtue.
High Virtue makes no fuss and has no private ends
to serve:
Low Virtue not only fusses but has private ends to
serve.
High humanity fusses but has no private ends to
serve:
High morality not only fusses but has private ends
to serve.
High ceremony fusses but finds no response;
then it tries to enforce itself with rolled - up sleeves.

Failing Tao, man resorts to Virtue.
Failing Virtue, man resorts to humanity.
Failing humanity, man resorts to morality.
Failing morality man resorts to ceremony.
Now ceremony is the merest husk of faith and loyalty;

**It is the beginning of all confusion and disorder.
As to fore knowledge, it is only the flower of Tao,
and the beginning of folly.
Therefore, the full-grown man sets his heart
upon the substance rather than the husk;
Upon the fruit rather than the flower.
Truly he prefers what is within to what is without.**

Does a child have virtue?...........no.....he does not even know such a thing exists...

Does a child have no virtue?............again 'no' is the answer

Then, what does a child have that makes him joyous?

He has 'nothing' .... 'nothing' makes him/keeps him happy...

it is his nature to be joyous......unless hungry or sick...

I was also a child many decades ago...

I must have also enjoyed having 'nothing'..

Now I have so much, but where is my joy?

When I was a child, my joy was a twin brother of 'nothing'....

As I grew up, my misery is the twin brother of having many things...

such paradox...the unfortunate truth of life....

Country, culture, community decided about my life as to what I should wear, when and how.

Restrictions more on me, being a female.

I was fed with 'right living' and 'right conduct' according to the group I belonged to.

Over feeding made me sick...I vomited...

I cleansed myself of all extra calories dumped on me...

I gave myself wings...I broke away from my religion... my gurus and my family...

I have no body but everybody is mine...

A strange happening indeed...difficult to explain....but makes living easier...for me as well as for others...

no demands...no commands ....

Because I have tasted freedom, I let others enjoy their freedom.

freedom has no fear...either of life or of death...

All rules and regulations, the do's and don'ts, are mainly for women.

Is there any restriction or code of conduct for men?... almost nil...

I call men 'weaker sex' for they fear the mental power and intelligence of females. She runs the family, looks after the elderly and the sick, sacrifices much for her family and yet does her work silently.

As discussed in a previous chapter, there are religious ceremonies from birth to death.

Why so many ceremonies? I have no answer...

Lao Tzu calls 'ceremonies' as husk.

The husk is a protective layer for what is inside.

Inside all ceremonies is the strong message of being "Happy"...our Original self!

We have forgotten "HAPPINESS"..

That is why we cling to ceremonies...

rituals become important...

Whatever is forced on us, makes us rebel against such system. There are people, who just follow others ...some do it as a part of social or religious obligation and few others play safe by just blindly following the system and the custom. Why antagonize anybody?

This is the main cause of having many religions.

Before religions were born, man was born.

But the first born (the humans) is given less importance and the second born (religions) is given maximum importance.

Religions become organizations. Organizations have to run. To run you need money. To get money you must do business. The easiest business is to 'create fear".

You can create real fear by using weapons or psychological fear by creating 'heaven' and 'hell'.

Converting people at gun points happens everywhere.

This beautiful earth can be made into a massive grave yard. There will not be anybody to mourn us.

Who will mourn whom?

39th Verse

HUMILITY IS DIVINITY

From of old there are not lacking things that has attained Oneness.
The sky attained Oneness and became clear;
The earth attained Oneness and became calm;
The spirits attained Oneness and became charged with mystical powers;
The fountains attained Oneness and became full;
The ten thousand creatures attained Oneness and became reproductive;
Barons and princess attained Oneness and became sovereign rulers of the world.
All of them are what they are by virtue of Oneness.
If the sky were not clear, it would be likely to fall to pieces;
If the earth were not calm, it would be likely to burst into bits;
If the spirits were not charged with mystical powers, they would be likely to cease from being.

If the fountains were not full, they would likely to be dry up;
If the ten thousand creatures were not reproductive, they would be likely to come to extinction;
If the barons and princess were not the sovereign rulers, they would be likely to stumble and fall.
Truly, humanity is the root from which greatness springs
and the high must be built upon the foundation of the low.
That is why barons and princess style themselves "The Helpless One",
"the Little One" and "the Worthless One".
Perhaps they too realize their dependence upon the lowly.
Truly too much honour means no honour.
It is not wise to shine like jade and resound like stone chimes.

Lao Tzu's inspiration and explanation of profound wisdom comes from observing nature.

He says that the sky laden with cloud falls on earth as rain. Thus the sky becomes clear again so that in due course it can accommodate new clouds.

The rain that falls on the earth becomes one with the earth.

The water thus received by the earth is consumed by all the living beings and thus water becomes one with all of us.

The earthquakes also quieten after some time.

Every minute, every second, something is happening around us. There is constant movement.

A tiny little seed grows into a huge tree. The little seed contains in it the Tao which makes it grow as a sapling, then a tree with leaves, flowers and fruits.

People's faith in Divinity is as diverse as the creation itself. Some people have faith in idol worship, for some, it is their Holy books and for some, it is spirits.

While talking on spirits who are worshipped by people, where do they get their mystical powers from?

They get it from the Source of All....The Tao...

Many great saintly poets of India used to call themselves 'slaves'... 'servants' and also as 'beggers'. Saint poetess Meera calls herself a 'dasi' ..a female servant.

Sai Baba of Shirdi (worshipped by millions as God incarnate) used to say 'Allah Malik hai".; meaning; God is the Master (that means, I am His servant and just an instrument in executing His Divine Will).

Servants and slaves do their master's bidding.

A beggar is dependent on others.

If Sai Baba had no body to recognize His greatness, He would never been installed in so many temples for people to worship. God's glory is revealed through His devotees.!

Thus, the "Big" has its foundation on the "small".

The Master also says that barons and kings (the rulers) attained that state because of people under him. The 'above' people are "above" because of people "below" them. Thus 'the lowly give rise to the powerful'.

In referring to people with power and money like princes and barons, is Lao Tzu referring to royalties and rich people according to ordinary sense of the terms?

To my understanding, the barons and royalties that the master is referring to are the people who live according to virtue. Such people are the real sovereign rulers of the world. People who rule by treachery or tormenting people can never be 'sovereign rulers of the world'. As to the barons, if they had taken to unethical way for massing wealth, they would also be not referred to as 'sovereign rulers.".

Lao Tzu stands for highest virtue in all our activities. To stand by virtue, we must stabilize ourselves. To stabilize ourselves, we must live according to Greatest Virtue (Tao or God).

"Seek thee first the kingdom of God" is the message.

Therefore, the Master says:

That is why barons and princes style themselves 'the helpless one'..the 'little one' and the 'worthless one.'

Lao Tzu's message is always full of paradoxes. The opposite exists simultaneously.

The inseparable twins smile at us every time we read his verses.

The 'small' becomes 'big'

Not seeking anything makes you rich.

Living by Great Virtue you defy death.

40th Verse

MYSTERY REVEALED

The movement of the Tao consists in Returning.
The use of the Tao consists in softness.
All things under heaven are born of the corporeal:
The corporeal is born of the Incorporeal.

As discussed in an earlier chapter, Hindus have two main schools of Philosophical thought...advaita and dwaita.

Advaita is about 'oneness' of the soul and God...as propagated mainly by Adi Shankaracharya.

Dwaita says that God is the Supreme being and that the individual soul is different from it.(Dwaita was propagated by exalted personalities like Madhvacharya, Andal etc.)

Shakaracharya says in his "nirvanashatak"...I am neither my mind, nor my intelligence nor my ego...I. I am pure Bliss...Pure Bliss...Pure Bliss.. I am Shiva.. I am Shiva.. I am Shiva...(the Auspicious One). In such a divine condition, there is no need for rituals and other paraphernalia associated with it.

The devotion that has merged itself into All that has no other way of expressing the inexpressible.

Dwaita form of devotion keeps God as an object of worship. The freedom enjoyed by such devotee is tremendous. God can be your child, mother, friend, your master or lover. This is called as navavidha bhakthi.(nine ways of relating to God). It follows, naturally, that there are ceremonies from early morning till mid night.

God is woken up in the morning...the decorations used the previous day are removed...a holy bath is given...new dress (vastra) is wrapped around him...He is decorated head to foot. Then he is offered bhog (prasadam or food). At night they sing to Him and put Him to sweet slumber.

There is music and music from morning till night.

Who would like to come out of it?

Adwaita is incorporeal..

dwaita is corporeal...

When we understand Lao Tzu, we will also understand the inseparable nature of Form and Formless..

Form is born from the Formless.

Bhagvad Gita:13.30. When he sees the separate existence of all beings inherent in the One, and their expansion from That (one) alone, he then becomes Brahman (enlightened)

41st Verse

APPEARANCES CAN BE DECEPTIVE

When a wise scholar hears the Tao,
he practices it diligently.
When a mediocre scholar hears the Tao,
he wavers between belief and unbelief.
When a worthless scholar hears the Tao,
he laughs boisterously at it.
But if such a one does not laugh at it,
the Tao would not be the Tao!

The wise men of old truly said,
The bright Way looks dim.
The progressive Way looks retrograde.
The smooth Way looks rugged.
High Virtue looks like an abyss.
Great whiteness looks spotted.
Abundant Virtue looks deficient.
Established Virtue looks shabby.
Solid Virtue looks as though melted.
Great squareness has no corners.

Great talents ripen late.
Great sound is silent.
Great form is shapeless.

The Tao is hidden and nameless;
Yet it alone knows how to render help and to fulfill.

Indian philosophy, (especially Bhagavad Gita) classifies people mainly under three categories according to their tendencies i.e. Satva, Rajas and Tamas.

Satva people perform all allotted duties as an offering to God. They have no likes or dislikes. They are impartial. They feel themselves to be the instruments of God and as such shun publicity and take no credit for their achievements. They have no ego at all.

Rajas type of people are motivated for achievement for they want to prove themselves superior to others. Their work is ego-based.

Tamas people are at the lowest level of consciousness for they have no sense of judgment. They do not think about the consequences of their action for many times they indulge in destroying others.

A similar classification is given by Lao Tzu about people.

when a wise scholar hears the Tao, he practices it diligently.

The satvic person lives the life in accordance with Tao. His simplicity, his way of dealing with life and the challenges that go with it, his attitude of not desiring any credit to his achievements are the invisible assets he possesses.

when a mediocre scholar hears the Tao, he wavers between belief and unbelief.

The mediocre type of people oscillates between belief and doubt. They will be swinging and swaying. Any misfortune in their lives, they will blame God. But when they achieve something, they will unashamedly take credit for every achievement that fall in their lap.

They tell God; "Head I win.....tail you lose".

The last category of people whom Lao Tzu calls as "worthless" will only mock at people's faith in the Supreme Power.

when a worthless scholar hears the Tao, he laughs boisterously at it.

The atheists deny God. To deny something, you indirectly accept its existence!

but if such a one does not laugh at it, the Tao would not be the Tao.

Indian mythology is replete with stories that reveal the power of God who manifests Himself when a person totally depends of Him.

Manifesting need not necessarily be in some physical form.

A story from the life of great poet saint Mirabai is worth a mention here.

Mirabai the great devotee was poisoned by her own people. What was her crime? She renounced her royal status and broke away from family life and surrendered to her Lord Krishna. Her husband and in-laws sneered at her devotion and felt she was a black sheep in the royal household and must be punished by poisoning her to death.

Here God manifests as a miracle that made the poison inactive and ineffective.

Mirabai's total surrender would never be known to the world, but for that incident.

A person who is absorbed totally in God looks different from the majority of us. In their ecstasy of being with God, they hardly know the way of the world.

When Ramakrishna Paramahamsa saw black clouds, he would go into ecstatic dance. The reason was that the cloud, for him, would resemble Goddess Kali whom he worshipped.

This deep love for the divine, looks like madness to people of the world.

There are many exalted personalities who lived only for God. Only a few of them were recognized for their greatness while they were alive.

Not that they cared about recognition.....

42ⁿᵈ Verse

THE INSEPERABLE TWINS

Tao gave birth to One,
One gave birth to Two,
Two gave birth to Three,
Three gave birth to all the myriad things.

All the myriad things carry the Yin on their backs and
hold the Yang in their embrace.
Deriving their vital harmony from the proper
blending
of the two vital Breaths.

What is more loathed by men than to be "helpless",
"little", and "worthless"?
And yet these are the very names the princess and
barons
call themselves.

Truly, one may gain by losing;
And one may lose by gaining.

What another has taught let me repeat:
"A man of violence will come to a violent end".
Whoever said this can be my teacher and my father.

Tao gave birth to One,
One gave birth to Two,
Two gave birth to Three,
Three gave birth to all the myriad things.
All the myriad things carry the Yin on their backs
and
hold the Yang in their embrace.
Deriving their vital harmony from the proper blending
of the two vital Breaths.

According to Hindu philosophy, before creation was a Great Void and everything came into existence from that Void. This Supreme Power created Brahma and He (Brahma) in turn created the world. This concept is described in some earlier chapter as well. As we have positive, negative and neutral in electricity working together, we have Brahma the creator, Vishnu the sustainer and Shiva the destroyer. The One Supreme Power creates, maintains and destroys. The three main classification of God is for lay person like many of us to understand the Oneness behind all actions that take place.

According to *Dwaita* philosophy, the concept of God is explained as a potter molding earthen pots and pans as per his wish. This is the philosophy of 'two'.....the potter and his clay.

Adwaita, the philosophy of Non-dualism or 'one' says, the clay molds itself by itself and destroys itself ...this goes on and on...just clay...just a play...Hindus call it *Leela* or divine drama. In drama there is no reality. Everybody just plays his or her allotted role and quits.

The Unmanifest (One) becomes Manifest (two). The Manifest becomes three (*Maya* or illusion). What is the illusion? All forms are illusion, since the underlying principle is *Aatma* or Soul. As explained in some other chapter, gold is the essence of gold ornament - bangles, rings or chains that are made are just the different forms of the same essence. Illusion should not be misunderstood in a mundane manner as we experience during a magic show.

Lao Tzu goes in numerical sequence of one, two, three. After that he says; 'myriad things'. Yin is female or negative and yang is male or positive. When yin and yang energy is balanced, there is better physical, mental and emotional health which are as important to spiritual seekers as to worldly people. The Hindu God Ardhanareeshwar (a two-in-one form of Lord Shiva with His Consort Parvati) is another way of expressing the yin and yang principle. Shiva is on the right side while Parvati, His consort, occupies the left side. According to yoga texts, breathing from the left side nostril activates ida nadi(channel). This is cool and related to moon. The right side nostril breathing is activates the pingala nadi(channel) and is related to sun or warmth. Sushumna nadi runs in between them and is considered to be important in spiritual development. This energy balance is represented beautifully in Bharatnatyam where the dancers adore themselves with many ornaments. They wear a crescent moon shaped ornament on the left and on right they have a circular ornament representing the sun on their head. The central portion of the head is decorated with another ornament representing the sushumna. This vertical band is secured in such a way that the more decorative part touches the beginning of the hairline or forehead. Balancing of emotions is important to all of us. It becomes all the more important to a spiritual seeker and certain types of pranayama help them to achieve this balance of mind in subtle yet very deep way.

> **What is more loathed by men than to be "helpless", "little", and "worthless"?**
> **And yet these are the very names the princess and barons**
> **call themselves.**
> **Truly, one may gain by losing;**
> **And one may lose by gaining.**

Nobody likes to depend on others, for it makes one feel small and worthless. Our ego will fight against such belittling feelings till the last. For many elderly people, the very idea of them becoming dependent on somebody makes them feel miserable. Many prefer death than dependency.

Lao Tzu says that 'princess and barons' called themselves as 'helpless' 'little' and 'worthless. A prince is from a royal family but he depends on so many people around him. All the riches that he enjoys are a result of many people toiling behind him. Similarly, a baron, a flourishing merchant, depends on his suppliers and customers for his business to prosper. Thus we see inter-dependency in all walks of our lives.

Lao Tzu in his inimitable style tells us that no man is an island. In fact, higher the position in our lives, greater seems to be the dependency on others. The prince as well as well as the baron, in a way, depend on ordinary citizens. A prince has less freedom of movement or speech. Everything has to be measured and marked. The baron, (the business tycoon) has to be extra nice to his customers for which he has to lower himself. In politics, this drama of being over-nice can be seen just before the elections.

Coming down from their high-pedestal, according to the master's perspective is to 'lose' something.

A student spends hours to get good marks. He has lost time, lost some sleep and other entertaining activities but gained good marks! This is applicable in every walk of life. Let us think over and create our own balance sheets. Loss and gain, the negative and the positive exists everywhere simultaneously.

What another has taught let me repeat:
"A man of violence will come to a violent end".
Whoever said this can be my teacher and my father.

A man of wisdom will never claim any knowledge to be his own. Great teachers never claim originality of their teachings. Enlightened persons conducting *satsang* (spiritual congregation) will always give all the credit to their gurus. Krishna, the World Teacher, while guiding Arjuna in the battle field of Kurukshetra tells Arjuna that He will teach about 'yoga puratanah', which means ancient yoga. Even the Lord makes no claim to the divine knowledge that He imparted! Such humility He had!!

43rd Verse

EFFORTLESS EFFORT

The softest of all things
overrides the hardest of all things.
Only Nothing can enter into no-space.
Hence I know the advantages of Non-Ado.
Few things under heaven are as instructive as
the lesson of Silence,
Or as beneficial as the fruits of Non-Ado.

This world is millions of years old. It has been running even before we were born. It will continue to do so even if we do not exist. While working in an orphanage, I have seen new born surviving great sickness though a typical home-care was absent. Till three years ago, my husband used to run the family. Then, he decided to quit the game. Like many Indian women, I had lived a protected life. Now I live alone. Who is running my home now? The invisible Tao makes things happen.

How can I repay Tao? There is no way, yet, I found my own way of serving His creation. While doing so, I take no credit. While doing so, I do not expect anything in return. I do not expect even a word of thanks from the people I work for. I work alone and He sends the people to help me do my humble offering. Silence is not just absence of words ...words are just external. Real silence is internal: when the mind stops demanding particular result, you are in silence. When two similar things merge, there will be just one. When two dissimilar things mix, say 'x' and 'y', the result will be totally different. It will neither be just 'x' nor 'y'.

To merge in 'Tao' we should be like 'Tao'...no likes...no dislikes...no doership...no expectation...

This is non-doing doing or the essence of karma yoga. When you do not 'do', you do everything. Words become inadequate and the person goes in silence. In that silence, he meets Him.

44th Verse

CEILING ON DESIRES

As for your name and your body, which is the dearer?
As for your body and your wealth, which is the more
to be prized?
As for gain and loss, which is more painful?

Thus, an excessive love for anything will cost you
dear in the end.
The storing up of too much good will entail a heavy
loss.
To know when you have enough is to be immune
from disgrace.
To know when to stop is to be preserved from perils.
Only thus can you endure long.

What is dearest to us? Our wealth, name and fame
and all that we have is because of having a human body. If
this body dies, to whom will the wealth belong? What will
happen to the so called glory we achieved while alive? Every

achievement is because of this living body. As such, our body deserves every respect and care we can give till the last breath. Which is the most vital process of our body? It is the process of breathing which starts at birth and stops at death. So, we need to be aware and careful for every breath we take. Once the breathing stops, it cannot be brought back.

We usually put this body in great turmoil for amassing wealth. Who knows how much wealth is enough? When there is too much wealth, man has to face dangers from robbers. He has to worry about protecting his hard earned wealth. We cannot eat two days' quota of food in one go. But we think of hoarding food (and wealth) for two generations!! Enjoying physical pleasures, man exhausts his human body and he goes to sleep. But in his sleep, his mind seems to be working and sets up a plan for the next exploration. Listening to the insatiable desires of the mind, the man's body finally gives up and various types of diseases eat him up slowly. Actually, the body mechanism intuitively knows when to stop. Unfortunately, we are not in tune with our own body, our own nature. Our mind has not learnt its lesson in spite of living with the body for so long!! What a pitiable state it is in. I strongly feel we should learn from the body...it has some great practical lessons to teach us.

45th Verse

MIND IS A MIRROR

The greatest perfection seems imperfect,
and yet its use is inexhaustible.
The greatest fullness seems empty,
and yet its use is endless.

The greatest straightness looks like crookedness.
The greatest skill appears clumsy.
The greatest eloquence sounds like stammering.

Restlessness overcomes cold,
but calm overcomes heat.

The peaceful and serene
is the norm of the world.

In our enthusiasm to make things better, we fiddle
with nature. We try our hands at cross breeding animals,
vegetables, fruits and crops. A cub born to a tiger and lion

was called as tigon. Should it behave like a tiger or live like a lion? Though both of them are flesh-eating animals, their behavior is quite different.

I also remember a vegetable called pomato....a cross breed of tomato and potato. Can I eat it raw like a tomato or cook and eat like a potato? Best way is to eat potato and tomato... both are tasty! Seedless variety of fruits (papaya and grapes) are considered as a big breakthrough. My guru used to say that such fruits devoid of seeds are barren and cannot be used for reproduction purposes. That which is not useful in re-producing it's own species is supposed to be as good as dead. In some gardens, we see the gardeners trimming and pruning trees and shrubs to give it a particular shape and height. We also see forms of animals and birds created by these creative gardeners.

Just imagine for a moment, if all of us look alike, what would our condition be? It would be like the Hindi movie I watched. The name of the movie was "Robot" (robot in Hindi and *Yandiran* in Tamil). There are thousands of people with the same physical features and there is confusion and chaos.

If everybody sang exactly like Lata Mangeshkar, we will be bored. To enjoy soothing music, the people should listen in silence. Of course there are other types of music which makes you dance or tap your feet. To put a child to sleep, the mother does not sing feet-tapping songs. She knows that soft music, the lullabies, will soothe her child into sweet, serene slumber. Sing soothing music to the world and give them peace and rest. This music is silent...yes! Silence is what want we have to cultivate in our hearts.

Inner silence and outer activity is a divine combination which will benefit all.

46ᵗʰ Verse

GODLESS SOCIETY

When the world is in possession of Tao,
the galloping horses are led to fertilize the fields
with their droppings.
When the world has become Taoless,
war horses breed themselves on the suburbs.
There is no calamity like not knowing what is
enough.
There is no evil like covetousness.
Only he who knows what is enough will always have
enough.

When the world was filled with Tao or Divinity, the horses moved in the 'field' of Tao. They did not go astray. Because of such closeness to Tao, even the droppings had their usefulness to fertilize the lands. As everything was centered on Tao, nothing was wasted or disregarded. When the horses (our sense organs) moved away from Tao (God or Spirit), we were lured by the pleasures of flesh. We moved away from the Supreme Power, the source of everything.

Like a dog trying to catch its own tail by going round and round, we go in circles called repeated births and repeated deaths. With every birth, more and more karmas are accumulated as every unfulfilled desire leads to repeated births.

Feeding the hungry is considered a holy task in many religions. When you feed a hungry person, after some time, he will not be able to eat more. He feels 'full'...even if it is for few hours only. Anything other than food will not give such feeling of 'enough'.

A satisfied heart is close to God. When you satisfy a hungry stomach, you are helping that person to get closer to god...at least temporarily!

A house has a ceiling but man's desire has no ceiling. If there is no ceiling to the house, rains, storms, snow, dust storm, and every possible calamity will enter it.

Lao Tzu says: "there is no evil like covetousness". Devils or evil characters are symbolically depicted with long nails or claws, canine teeth, horns on their heads to butt their enemies, their eyes flaming red and the tongues hang out as though to gobble up anything that come their way. Thus every part conveys terror.

The Master (Lao Tzu) advises us to look into our lives and have a ceiling on our desires in order to live a life of peace and contentment. This is true worship, this is true happiness.

47th Verse

THE INWARD JOURNEY

Without going out of your door,
you can know the ways of the world.
Without peeping through your window,
you can see the Way of Heaven.
The farther you go, the less you know.

Thus the Sage knows without travelling,
sees without looking,
and achieves without Ado

We know, either by our personal experience, or through some friends or books, that there are people who have psychic power. They read our past and predict our future. Many people take guidance from them.

This is the age of science and technology. Sitting at home, we can communicate with people from any part of the world. New inventions are pouring into our lives. Our computers and smart phones are wonderful machines in our hands. We cannot think of our lives without them. Let us do a bit of going back in time...hundreds of years ago. Hindu scriptures describe about weapons which never miss their targets. We come across people who used to do aerial travel. When Mahabharata war was going on, Sanjaya gave a running commentary on the happenings to the blind king Dhritarashtra sitting far away from the battle field. These are special abilities gained through some esoteric practices. What special qualities these people had, which, we do not seem to posses? Living in solitude, going deep in meditation can open the doors to greater and greater knowledge of various aspects of life.

There have been seers who knew about the movements of celestial beings and gave exact dates of solar and lunar eclipses that would take place in the distant future.

When you have to travel miles and miles on a desert, you have only the stars and moon to guide your path. The very vastness and doing nothing except travelling probably gave them power to understand nature and its secrets. Unknowingly, they were meditating...doing nothing while doing something (travelling). Doing and non-doing thus happened without ado. When you are with nature, all alone by yourself, nature starts whispering secret, sacred knowledge. The sages and saints of India never set up any laboratory, there was apparently no hard labour either. They made themselves available to nature by having minimum contact with the world outside and thus received divine knowledge. If our brain is over-crowded with conflicts and confusion, even day to day activity will seem to be heavy load on our heads..

A scientist, like a saint, wants to know some secrets. The only difference is that a scientist takes help of external things whereas a saint takes the help of all-pervading Tao by going into or being in silence. ...the first is labour-intensive, whereas the second is love-intensive!

How to tap the All- pervading Wisdom?

Lao Tzu says: "The farther you go, the less you know.".

Why only a few people seem to have access to the wisdom of Tao, when Tao is impartial? The answer is: we are not anchored in Tao...we are not close to Tao.

What is Tao? It is LOVE AND LOVE ALONE... We cling to people and things that we love. Our whole energy seems to revolve around them. How do the million and trillion of galaxies stay together? The only energy is the energy of Supreme Love...unimaginable, unconditional, unsullied, undivided, eternal, causeless Love. When such a love develops in our hearts, we are close to Tao.

Otherwise we are away from God whom we worship in so many ways.

thus the sage knows without travelling,
sees without looking,
and achieves without ado

"Travelling" is moving towards worldly things leaving behind Tao.

Travelling is not to be understood in just physical sense of movement.

The master Lao Tzu takes us into the deep chambers of saints who achieved many things without doing anything and going nowhere.

———◆———

48th Verse

THE ULTIMATE VICTORY

Learning consists in daily accumulating;
the practice of Tao consists in daily diminishing.

Keep on diminishing and diminishing,
until you reach the state of Non-Ado.
No-Ado and yet nothing is left undone.

To win the world, one must renounce all.
If one still has private ends to serve,
One will never be able to win the world.

Let me tell you a story. The great Guru (Master) Adi Shankaracharya was walking along the banks of river Ganga where he found an old man trying to learn Sanskrit grammar by rote. The Guru was amused at the futility of that man's endevour, as no information or knowledge is going to help him in his final journey. Instead of remembering God, the ignorant man was trying to learn grammar. Thus was born

"Bhaja Govindam"..a very melodious, easy to learn song on the futility of human life devoid of divinity.

Lord Buddha and Lord Mahavira were princes before they attained enlightenment.

They renounced their kingdom in search of answers to the questions as to why there was so much suffering and how to get out of it.

We worship them not because they were kings. We worship them because they renounced their kingdoms. Their images of being sky-clad is the ultimate message of total renunciation. I bow my head in great reverence to these exalted personalities that have descended on this earth to redeem humanity.

As kings, they had ruled over a few people of their kingdom who lived at that time. After attaining enlightenment, they are ruling the hearts of the people all over the world even now. After relinquishing ordinary kingdom, they found Divine Kingdom. They have conquered the world not by waging war but with their unconditional love and compassion which arose out of the state of ultimate knowledge. They being physically absent has made no difference to their devotees, as they carry on the message of love and peace throughout the world for centuries. This, I feel, is immortality.

<hr>

49th Verse

INNOCENCE OF INFANTS

The Sage has no interest of his own,
but takes the interest of the people as his own.
He is kind to the kind;
He is also kind to the unkind:
For Virtue is kind.
He is faithful to the faithful;
He is also faithful to the unfaithful;
For Virtue is faithful.

In the midst of the world, the Sage is shy and self–effacing.
For the sake of the world he keeps his heart in its nebulous state.
All the people strain their ears and eyes:
The Sage only smiles like an amused infant.

We are good to our family and friends. It is natural to love our family. This love is mutual. Can we love people who do not like us or hate us? Not just difficult...but seems impossible too! We are loyal to people who are loyal with us. Can we still be loyal if the other person is not loyal? That too seems impossible. We change like chameleons which changes its colour according to the surroundings. That happens not by its will, but some superior intelligence giving protection in some manner for preservation of the species.

We have free will and yet, we are not chameleons. What is the reason? Is nature different to different people? The sun shines on Ganga water as well as the on the drainage water. Nature makes no distinction. God makes no distinction, either.

That is why nature is God. When you live like 'nature', showing no preferences or distinction, you reveal your original power...power of your source..the source of everything. Krishna says in Bhagwad Gita, Chapter VI – 30

"He who sees Me in all things and see all things in Me, he never becomes separated from Me, nor do I become separated from him."

This is man becoming God!

In the midst of the world, the Sage is shy and self–effacing.

For the sake of the world he keeps his heart in its nebulous state.

All the people strain their ears and eyes:

The Sage only smiles like an amused infant.

Lao Tzu, unlike many saints and sages who prefer solitude and advocate the same to spiritual seekers, gives subtle and indirect messages to us as to how to live and lead our lives centered on Tao. Why is he amused? He is amused because he sees people around him making frantic efforts all through their lives seeking and searching for happiness as though it lies only in the future. In spite of knowing the futility of such frenzied activity, he never passes judgment on people nor does he give unsolicited advice to them. That is why he is referred as being 'shy' and 'self-effacing'. Unsolicited advice sometimes silently screams: "I know better...you better listen to me"!

The unsullied heart of a sage has no impressions imprinted in his being. Like an infant, who has no past and no future which are just mind-related reference points, he also has no past and no future. He does not brand anybody and that makes him grander still. As his heart is in a nebulous state, he easily accepts everybody and every situation and at the same time actively participates doing his duty towards the society.

50th Verse

ETERNAL LIFE

When one is out of Life, one is in Death.
The companions of life are thirteen;
the companions of death are thirteen;
and when a living person moves into the Realm of Death,
his companions are also thirteen.
How is this? Because he draws upon the resources of Life too heavily.

It is said that he who knows well how to live meets no tigers or wild buffaloes on his road,
and comes out from the battle- ground untouched by the weapons of war.
For, in him, a buffalo would find no butt for his horns,
a tiger nothing to lay his claws upon,
and weapon of war no place to admit its point.
How is this?
Because there is no room for Death in him..

When one is out of Life, one is in Death
The companions of life are thirteen;
the companions of death are thirteen;

Lao Tzu says that in life and death our companions are thirteen. According to Indian philosophy, we are composed of 5 sense organs, five organs of cognition and the three invisible faculties called mind, intelligence and ego. That totals it up to thirteen. May be Lao Tzu is trying to tell us nothing really changes after death. Though the dead person is physically not visible, he lives in other realms not perceivable to our naked eyes. Many people have done a lot of research into the life after death and have shared their views about the eternity of life. This is the principle of re-incarnation. Osho used to say that death is like sleep. We are the same person when we get up in the morning the next day. A musician will be a musician before and after sleep. Since death is compared to sleep, the person will be born with the same tendencies in his next life as well. Child prodigy is strong proof of such phenomena. Lao Tzu also explains about the reason for such repeated births and deaths. The reason, according to him, is because the person is drawing heavily on resources. The resources are the unquenchable desire of the mind. There seems no end to his desires which makes him seek more and more from the world through his sense organs.

What is eternal life? Does eternal life mean people will not die? Even one second of deathlessness will destroy the world. So, what is 'eternal life'?

Lord Krishna, in Bhagwad Gita, explains beautifully about this phenomenon of being deathless.

2.23. The Lord says: "This (Self), weapons cut not; This, fire burns not: This, water wets not; and this wind dries not."

2.24: This Self cannot be cut, nor burnt, nor wetted nor dried. Changeless, all-pervading, unmoving, the Self is eternal.

2.25 This (Self) is said to be unmanifested, unthinkable and unchangeable. Therefore, knowing This to be such, thou oughtest not to mourn.

Immortality of soul is what the Lord is referring about. Though the body does all the work, whether good or bad, it is the life force inside us that does all the function. A dead man has all the organs in its respective places, but it cannot function as the life force has left the body.

Even a newly hatched chick runs helter-skelter trying to protect itself from being harmed or killed. If a chick has so much concern about self-preservation, how much should we humans have? Many people believed that mummifying the bodies of dead people will help them in resurrection at a later date. So far, not even one dead person has come out of grave alive. We are not debating about people with supernatural power bringing back a dead person to life like Lord Buddha or Jesus did. Krishna describes about the elements of nature having no effect on the 'atma' or 'soul'. He says, fire cannot burn, wind cannot dry, weapons cannot destroy ...the soul is immortal.

Lao Tzu being deeply in love with nature says:

"a buffalo would find no butt for his horns."
"a tiger nothing to lay his claws upon."
"weapon of war no place to admit its point."

Krishna says that as we change our dress, we change our bodies (after death).

2.22. The Lord says: "Even as a man casts off worn out clothes, and puts on others which are new, so the embodied casts off worn-out bodies, and enters into others which are new."

Krishna also says in the next verse 2.23 "This Self, weapons cut not; This, Fire burns not; This water wets not; and This wind dries not;

Death is as simple as that...just changing our garment.

That must be reason why a dead man is given a bath by his relatives before he is consumed to flames or buried. It is a common practice in India, especially among Hindus.

Osho, the mystic from India used to say that celebrate death with joy. When the master passed away, his disciples danced on the streets of Pune. Surely we will miss the person who left us, but let us be grateful for his presence in our life. Thousands have been transformed by his different types of meditations and the power of his words. I happen to be one of them...in a very humble way...

51ˢᵗ Verse

VIRTUE IS VEILED

Tao gives them life, Virtue nurses them, matter shapes them, environment perfects them.
Therefore all things without exception worship Tao and do homage to Virtue.
They have not been commanded to worship Tao and do homage to Virtue.
But they always do so spontaneously.

It is Tao that gives them life:
It is Virtue that nurses them, grows them, fosters them and shelters them,
comforts them, nourishes them and covers them under her wings.

To give life but to claim nothing,
To do your work but set no store by it,
To be a leader, not a butcher, this is called hidden Virtue.

Lao Tzu says: Tao gives them life...According to this statement, all the living beings come from Tao; which means that living beings get their life force from Tao. Then what about non-living beings like the five elements or the sun, moon and the earth, and the millions and millions of stars and galaxies that exist in the cosmos? They also come from Tao. How such mind-blowing things exist without some Creator or Operator? Is there one such a Being?

In the Bhagwad Gita, detailed description of creation is given in chapter 11. Without going too much into this chapter, I shall just give one such description.

11.7. Lord says.... "see now, O Arjuna, in this, My body, the whole universe centered in one – including the moving and the unmoving – and all else that thou desirest to see."

It must have truly be mind blowing experience for Arjuna, for when Lord Krishna reveals His Cosmic Form (*Vishwaroopa*), Arjuna sees not just gods, demi-gods and other celestial beings but also ogres, demons and other such terrifying entities. Tao is omnipresent and as such everything is God expressed. A person like Lao Tzu sees everything as the Supreme Power pervading ...from the minutest atoms to mighty mountains. As such, it becomes natural that he reveres things around him and uses them judiciously. How many Lao Tzus are in this world at present? ..may be just a handful. The rest of the people are only waiting to exploit nature and plunder people. This is due to their selfishness and ignorance about the Supreme Power they so faithfully worship in so many ways. Lao Tzu equates selfish people with butchers. People breed different types of animals like goats, sheep, chickens etc. They look after them with great care and concern. The animals are fed well and looked after properly. They are giving such service to the animals so that they call sell their meat.

As against this, there are people who look after stray, sick and injured animals. They feed them and look after them with great care. There is no business involved in such service. They value life. Life in every form is Tao.

Looking after poor people, helping them according to one's capacity is Virtue. Looking after trees and environment is also Virtue. So, according to Lao Tzu, looking after creation is great Virtue. Such acts become greatest virtue, when we do not seek name, fame or money from such service. Selfless people are the real leaders....the rest are all traders...in trade, profit and loss both exist. When there is no trade, you just do it because you want to do it. You are the master and you are the servant....The greatest realization is "whatever you do, you are the first recipient"...others are just in queue... When you throw mud at somebody, your hands are the first recipient..Understanding divine law and implicitly abiding by it is freedom...true freedom.

What is virtue? A thief will not like another thief stealing money from him. A murderer will not like anybody trying to murder or harm him or his family members. When it comes to one self, a thief prefers honesty. When it comes to oneself, a criminal prefers compassion. Why is it so? It is because deep down everybody is just soul or god. All the bad qualities that we come across have been acquired later on, for whatever reasons.

As such, basically all of us are pure 'souls'. Goodness is what we are. We are born with it. Wickedness is like an adopted child. It is not our own. It is borrowed or adopted by the ego. Seek your real child.

52nd Verse

FROM CREATION TO CREATOR

All-under-Heaven have a common Beginning.
This Beginning is the Mother of the world.
Having known the Mother,
we may proceed to know her children.
Having known the children,
we should go back and hold on to the mother.
In so doing, you will incur no risk.
even though your body be annihilated.

Block all the passages!
Shut all the doors!
And to the end of your days you will not be worn out.
Open the passages !
Multiply your activities!
And to the end of your days you will remain helpless.

To see the small is to have insight.
To hold on to the weakness is to be strong.
Use the lights, but return to your insight.

Do not bring calamities upon yourself.
This is the way of cultivating the way of the Changeless.

When we see a kitten, we know that the mother must be a cat, even if we have not seen her. When we see a puppy, we know the mother to be a she–dog (bitch) even if we have not seen her.

Similar should be our vision when we see the world and its myriad forms. Even if we are not able to see the Mother (the Creator), we know the Mother.

Through the young ones we see the mother, as in the case of animals.

The only way to see the Creator is through His Creation. When such understanding dawns on us, we start respecting and protecting the creation, be it animals, birds, river or trees and all the million living beings of this world.

Lao Tzu says: **"Block all the passages"**: Our sense organs are the passages to the outer world. When we use them to just minimum, our energy is saved to a very great extent. This is achieved by meditation and understanding the impermanency of things. Self-control is advocated so that we conserve our energy. Whenever we feel unwell or low in energy, the first thing we do is to close our eyes. Our body has inherent wisdom to conserve its energy. This closing of eyes (when we are unwell) is like depositing 100 rupees so that we can withdraw 100 rupees. Thus we end up with nil balance.

On the contrary, when we close eyes and meditate for some time, our energy is preserved. You can withdraw this energy when you need it.

'Open all the passages":

Our sense organs are always in search for more. In this senseless search for more, it is exhausted and the body becomes weaker and drops down dead. Satisfying our sense organs is like trying to put out fire by adding fuel to it. Is Lao Tzu against enjoying the pleasures and beauty of this world? No. On the contrary, he is only asking us to know when and how to draw a line. Messages from masters are as mysterious as the masters themselves. Repeated reading, meditating over the messages is the only way to get even a glimpse of the profound wisdom contained therein.

"seeing the small is clarity"...

A man without prejudice will give importance even to a person doing menial work. Such a man is a man with 'clarity"...clarity of vision. In nature, everything depends on everything. Our house, roads and city are kept clean because of people doing menial jobs. Can we live without such 'small' people?

Keeping flexible is called strength.

We come across people who have strong likes and dislikes. Not just that, they will also try to influence others. Such dogmatic persons are disliked by others. Flexibility is the quality to step into others' shoes and see the situation from their perspective.

Such people are easy to get along with and are welcome wherever they go.

53rd Verse

FALSE RICHNESS

If only I had the tiniest grain of wisdom,
I should walk in the Great Way,
and my only fear would be to stray from it.

The Great Way is very smooth and straight;
and yet the people prefer devious paths.

The court is very clean and well garnished,
but the fields are very weedy and wild,
and the granaries are very empty!
They wear gorgeous clothes,
they carry sharp swords,
they surfeit themselves with food and drink,
they posses more riches than they can use!
they are heralds of brigandage!
As for Tao, what do they know about it?

There is a saying: fools tread where angels fear:...In this verse, Lao Tzu says that one need not be a scholar to understand the universal laws. Even a little understanding about this cosmic law, will lead us towards Tao or Great Light or God. "As you sow, so shall you reap"...is the only law of this world. Between two points, the shortest distance is always a straight line. Being straightforward in whatever we do, will keep us close to Tao. When we are close to Tao, we achieve many things effortlessly. People trust us and feel safe with us. Can there be a better blessing than this?

Only a fool will go astray and away from Tao. A ruler who has moved away from Tao will become ruthless. He will not be bothered about his people. Instead of trying to do some good for them, he will use his riches (which have actually come from them in the form of taxes etc.) only to satisfy himself.

A selfish, ruthless ruler will adorn himself with costly clothes and live a pompous life at the cost of his people.

The lifeless things like his palace and his beautiful court will hide the tragedy behind those glittering externals. The fields have withered away...very little vegetation is found... even the little vegetation that we see will not be of much use to humans, for only weeds and thistles grow. Such a ruler gives birth to 'brigands' which means chief of thieves! He has created thieves because of his misuse of his wealth and power. People under such a ruler wait for every opportunity to steal whatever they can! If only he had known Tao, he would never have gone astray.

54th Verse

BE THE BEACON OF LIGHT

What is well planted cannot be uprooted.
What is well embraced cannot slip away.
Your descendents will carry on the ancestral sacrifice
for generations without end.

Cultivate Virtue in your own person,
and it becomes a genuine part of you.
Cultivate in the family, and it will abide.
Cultivate it in the community, and it will live and
grow.
Cultivate it in the state, and it will flourish
abundantly.
Cultivate it in the world, and it will become universal.

Hence, a person must be judged as person;
A family as family;
A community as community;
A state as state,
The world as world.

How do I know about the world?
By what is within me.

Let me start with the second paragraph first......it reads...

Cultivate Virtue in your own person,
and it becomes a genuine part of you.
Cultivate in the family, and it will abide.
Cultivate it in the community, and it will live and
grow.
Cultivate it in the state, and it will flourish
abundantly.
Cultivate it in the world, and it will become universal.

There is an adage "charity begins at home". For me "charity begins from 'my' home"...

The first word is 'my'... refers to 'I'...hence 'my' comes first before the word 'home'. In other words 'practice' before you 'preach'. Whatever is repeatedly done becomes a habit. As we always influence each other in this world, like a farmer we have to cultivate ourselves.

A farmer does not sow the seeds which he does not want to harvest. In other words, he sows such seeds that he wishes to harvest after some time. In doing so, along with the grains he has planted, there grow some unwanted plants or weeds as well. He has to remove them carefully.

Our mind is also like a field. It is up to us to grow the crops we wish to harvest. Tomato seed will produce only tomatoes and not capsicum or for that matter any other plant. What do we want to harvest in life?

We desire peace, love, compassion and straightforwardness. This is the essence of the adage "charity begins at home".

In Tirukkural, the Sage Poet says: When people wonder what sort of good karma this man has done to beget such a son, it is the only way to repay our father.

(Hinduism is particular about taking care of our parents and bring good name to them).

What happens when a man goes astray? What happens when a man ruling the kingdom goes astray? There will be fight for supremacy which is decided in the battle field. Wars leave widows and orphans.

As there are less or no earning male members (having lost many in the wars), the females are forced into working. The opportunities of earning money that a female enjoys now were not there at all some hundreds of years ago. To support the family, she was forced into degrading herself. In fact, 'prostitution' is termed as the oldest profession in the world. The children born to such women suffer emotionally as the society ostracizes and rejects them. Instead of looking into circumstances which had lead the woman into such desperate action, these people are branded as 'fallen'. To 'raise' a family she had to 'fall'. Unfortunate indeed is her condition!

So, how should our actions be in our life..? Every deed is a seed indeed...Behind every deed is our 'mind' and the thoughts that arise from it. Hence, it is imperative that we cultivate our minds. Such noble qualities keep our family in great honour which percolates down to future generations as well.

How do I know the world? By what is within me. In my younger years, I was a great movie buff. I loved Tamil and Hindi movies very much. English movies were not my favorites. The hero or heroine, when in happy mood, will be singing and dancing in beautiful gardens with lots of trees and different types of flowers. When they were not together in love, the back ground will be in some desert region depicting the barrenness of their lives without their loved ones.

When we are with God or Tao, the world would look like a garden...

Without God, our life is barren...just thorns and thistles hurting us from all sides.

───◆◈◆───

55th Verse

PRISTINE PURITY

One who is steeped in Virtue is akin to the new-born babe.
Wasps and poisonous serpents do not sting it,
Nor fierce beast seize it,
Nor birds of prey maul it.
Its bones are tender, it sinuous soft, but its grip is firm.
It has not known the union of the male and the female,
growing in its wholeness, and keeping its vitality in
its perfect integrity.
It howls and screams all day long without getting hoarse,
because it embodies perfect harmony.
To know harmony is to know the Changeless.
To know the Changeless is to have insight.
To hasten the growth of life is ominous.
To control the breath by the will is to overstrain it.
To be overgrown is to decay.
All this is against Tao,
and whatever is against Tao soon ceases to be.

The most beautiful sound I have ever heard in my life was the first cry of my son. I am sure many mothers share my feelings. After the great agony and anxiety, to give birth to the baby is like being with the Creator, face to face.

Lao Tzu compares the innocence of enlightened people to that of new born babes. Pure, immaculate and unsullied by things around him, he exudes great joy. His every movement, even twisting and turning, and making grimaces is a sight to behold. He opens his eyes but does not see....does not see as you and I do. His vision is as pure as his being. His vision does not brand 'mine' and 'yours', 'rich and poor' 'known and unknown', 'male and female' and all other opposites that exists in us.

He is helpless and vulnerable to people around him. Why does Lao Tzu say **Wasps and poisonous serpents do not sting it.**

Lao Tzu cannot be referring to any real animals or birds. We know that no child can withstand the attack of ferocious animals and poisonous creatures. New born babies either sleep or cry. The ferocious animals and poisonous creatures are the negative human tendencies which Lao Tzu is referring to. Lust, greed, anger, jealousy, hatred, fear and other negative qualities are the 'ferocious animals and birds' tearing us apart, bit by bit, piece by piece. The Indian philosophy has the corresponding *Shadripus*, or the six internal enemies of man, corresponding to these negative qualities mentioned above. A saint–poet Valluvar from South India says 'People who have not heard the sound (babble) of their child will say that the sound of flute or Veena (a string instrument) is sweet. The greatest music is the cry of new born babies, especially to its mother and family. A child does not need breath control or pranayama, since it is able to breathe naturally. It is in tune with nature, and is naturally lively. A new born baby will only cry his lungs out. Yes...that is the reason why babies cry...to get more air into their lungs as there is no physical activity he can do except wriggling and crying. We also need more oxygen.... but we cannot cry or wriggle all day long like the little one.

Lao Tzu lived in nature where fresh air was available in plenty. We live in man-made structures most of our lives. Our sedentary life is one of the reasons for many ailments. For people who lead sedentary life, doing pranayam is one of the best options to oxygenate themselves. Lao Tzu advocates flowing with the current. In some way, our breathing can be compared to a river flowing. Let the in-breath and out-breath be deep, yet relaxed. When we try deep breathing, we unnecessarily tend to over-strain ourselves. It needs practice to balance relaxation along with deep breathing.

What happens when we overstrain ourselves? People involved in extreme physical fitness like athletics, weight lifting, boxing etc. develop many physical problems later on in their lives because of over straining themselves. This list also includes people from other extremely competitive sports like international games, gymnastics etc. When sports are equated with money, the harm due to over-strain can be heavy later on in our lives. There are several examples of sports persons who over-strained themselves to win titles but landed up with severe injuries or long-term disability.

❖

56th Verse

BEYOND HUMAN PERCEPTION

He who knows does not speak.
He who speaks does not know.
Block all the passages!
Shut all the doors!
Blunt all edges!
Untie all tangles!
Harmonize all lights!
Unite the world into one whole!
This is called Mystical Whole,
Which you cannot court nor shun,
Benefit not harm, honour not humble.
Therefore, it is the highest of the world.

Strange it may seem all the wars start with words. Families and relationship break because of words. The words become swords when used indiscriminately to break people especially on religious grounds. They are the harbingers of evil, messengers of death.

Angry, hateful words are compared to sharp edges which inflict injuries to others.

At the same time, words have great power to unite, harmonize and bring peace to the world we live in.

Whoever divides people on whatever basis, be it religion, race or language, is the messenger of death. Nowadays, "Hate words" are passed around at lightening speed because of technology. Technology in wrong hands has destroyed many lives.

In contrast to this, great people have recommended silence as a panacea to counter hate words. Ideally, this silence should be arising out of inclusion, trust, love, maturity and great wisdom, and it should not be a shutting-off silence. Silence has to be understood properly by common people like us, and not be taken literally.

One should take the silence in its proper sense. For example, a mother may be silent and non-reactive with her child either out of love or out of anger. True silence or divine silence can come out of love and total acceptance, irrespective of the actions of the opposite person. Silence coming out of anger is negative and not desirable.

It is called as cold war. There is indifference and lack of communication in such cold war.

This silence is locking up of emotions. When emotions are locked up, there is implosion...the physical body is also affected and in due course it appears as some disease. Angry and hateful words are explosions. They destroy lives and peace.

Divine silence happens when we feel a deep connection with the Creator. In that ocean of bliss, we feel related to every part of the Creation, even with the small and the big.

In that ocean of bliss, everything is smooth, soft and tender. In that state of mind, there is great harmony, peace and deep sense of belonging to One Big Family, with love being the basis of all relations, the common golden thread uniting every being.

There are various levels of silence, which only a Master can guide how to achieve.

57th Verse

LIFE IS AN ECHO

You govern a kingdom by normal rules;
you fight a war by exceptional moves;
but you win the world by letting alone.
How do I know that this is so?
By what is within me!

The more taboos and inhibitions there are in the
world,
the poorer the people become.
The sharper the weapons the people possess,
the greater confusion reigns in the realm.
The more clever and crafty the men,
the oftner strange things happen.
The more articulate the law as and ordinances,
the more robbers and thieves arise.

Therefore, the Sage says:
I do not make any fuss, and the people transform
themselves.

I love quietude and the people settle down in their regular grooves.
I do not engage myself in any thing,
and the people go rich.
I have no desires,
and the people return to Simplicity.

Rules and regulations were created when people strayed away from Tao, or Truth and started living a very selfish life. Lao Tzu says if we follow natural laws, there would be no need for artificial man-made laws. In some countries, only left hand driving is followed whereas in some countries, right hand driving is followed. Some countries have legalized abortions, same sex marriage, prostitution, pornography, gambling etc. Many such things are not allowed and strictly banned in other parts of the world.

Whatever it is, in the world, we will see that the more the number of laws, the more will be the law-breakers. Many times, we find that the law-makers are the biggest law breakers. So does it mean that we should not have laws? No. Lao Tzu is only trying to say that life is simple. Lao Tzu believes in leading a simple life respecting nature. Laws as such are made only for the purpose of making social life smooth, peaceful and harmonious. Rules are required to govern kingdoms.

The Sages are enlightened and self-realised souls. They are in tune with nature and everything else. Their presence and being is so strong, that people around them naturally become cohesive and peaceful. When we lead our life based on the principle of oneness, rules and regulations, in other words what is to be done and what is to be avoided will automatically follow. When the whole world is my family, where is the need to having rules and regulations? Yes... it looks like a utopian idea. Well; everything starts with an idea. Why not follow this 'idea'?

but you win the world by letting alone.

From this line, one can see that detachment is the key to Tao or Truth. Letting alone means being non-interfering, non-possessive. I am reminded of a beautiful Sanskrit word in Bhagwad Gita, which is 'sthitapragnya'. It means being totally established in one-self, Tao, truth or light.

The word Guru is very beautiful. The word 'gu' means 'darkness' and 'ru' means 'light'. A guru takes his people from darkness to light. In India, Guru is worshipped as God.

When we live in the light of Tao, we show the path to others living in darkness.

Such a person is called 'guru'. Unfortunately, there are fake gurus as well and it is very difficult to make out the difference from external appearances and spoken or written words. That is why it is said that guru searches for his disciple and a true devotee need not search for a guru. When the time is ripe, guru will find him. World is full of infectious diseases. I am not referring to the physical ailments. I am referring to the quagmire of desires, which are unending and like an infectious disease spread very fast.

There is a saying: "when you laugh, others also laugh... when you cry, you have to cry alone..." True in some sense, as nobody wants to be unhappy. When a person is all the time crying (having a forlorn face), cribbing and complaining, his friends slowly leave him. That is why he has to "cry alone." As our very nature is happiness, we are happy when people around us exude joy. The corollary is also true; when I am happy, I make others happy.

Every emotion has 'motion' inherent in it. It has a snowballing effect. Anger also gathers momentum and bursts as volcano when more people get into that trap.

In India, satsang or being in holy company is stressed to keep our emotions in harmony.

Lao Tzu says "I do not make any fuss, and the people transform themselves. I love quietude and the people settle down in their regular grooves." Many people have shared their experience of total positive change after being with a true master like Ramana Maharshi, the saint from Thiruvannamalai in South India. And he did nothing...

Why do we have rules and regulations? We need them because we have no control over our emotions and behavior. Children are curious and adventurous by nature. Naturally, it is the duty of people around them to tell them about dos and donts. A man with understanding and wisdom does not need such 'dos' 'don'ts.'

A warrior takes care of his weapons and always carries them. Why does a warrior, a brave man, need a weapon? Only weak persons need weapons for self protection. Whoever is carrying weapons indirectly reveals their weakness.

Lao Tzu destroys all our wrong understanding about the presumed bravery of soldiers who carry weapons. Laws are made after a great deal of discussion by people with legal background. Some crooks become even sharper and they find out loop holes to escape laws. Again people enact new rules to cover these loop holes... It is a never ending process... More laws...more crooks. Live naturally, in harmony with the Truth and by respecting creation, and you do not need man-made laws.

58ᵗʰ Verse

THE SAINTLY KING

Where the ruler is mum, mum,
the people are simple and happy.
Where the ruler is sharp, sharp,
the people are wily and discontented..

Bad fortune is what good fortune leans on,
good fortune is what bad fortune hides in.
Who knows the ultimate end of this process?
Is there no norm of right?
Yet what is normal soon becomes abnormal.
And what is auspicious soon turns ominous.
Long indeed have the people been in a quandary.

Therefore, the Sage squares without cutting,
carves without disfiguring,
straightens without straining.
enlightens without dazzling.

Lao Tzu says "where the ruler is mum mum…"

How can anybody rule without speaking?

"Actions speak louder than words"; We need such rulers who rule by setting themselves as an example for people to follow. When 'actions' speak, where is the need for eloquent speech as to what is to be done and what is not to be done?

This is the inner meaning of 'mum mum'…

Every law that is made will create something opposite to that – the law-breakers. That which is forced upon us will always be a burden to be discarded because that is not our natural state of being. The biggest farce is "peace keeping force". They have high tech killing machines and talk about 'peace'. We can only have a good laugh! It is akin to putting the weight on a pressure cooker. The steam seems to be contained inside the vessel, but only to build up more pressure.

A man of peace will not use 'pressure tactics' on his people. His very being is enough to bring about change of heart.

As discussed in the precious chapter (57), we all influence each other. It is imperative, therefore, to expand the circle of peace loving people by joining them.

Life is in cycles. Life is in pairs. Night follows day… day follows night..this is the law of nature. In the same context, Lao Tzu says, that good fortune is followed by bad fortune…bad fortune by good fortune… As such, a wise man remains unperturbed knowing this eternal, irrefutable law of nature. When such an expansion of intellect happens to a person, "sharp edges are smoothened without cutting"… he carves without disfiguring ..straightens without straining and enlightens without dazzling.

Let us create such a world …

B.G. 3.21: Whatsoever superior person does, that is followed by others. When he demonstrates by action, that people follow.

———◈———

59th Verse

SAGE IS SAGACIOUS

In governing people and in serving Heaven,
there is nothing like frugality.
To be frugal is to return before straying.
To return before straying is to have a double reserve
of Virtue.
To have a double reserve of Virtue is to overcome
everything.
To overcome everything is to reach an invisible
height.
Only he who has reached an invisible height can
have a kingdom.
Only he who has got the Mother of the kingdom can
last long.
This is the way to be deep- rooted and firm-planted
in the Tao,
the secret of long life and lasting vision.

Lao Tzu says: "In governing people and in serving heaven..."

A ruler immersed in virtue is actually serving Heaven or God while serving his people.

When such a ruler rules a country, where is the need to do so many rituals to appease Gods in Heaven? The master also says that "there is nothing like frugality"...

Unless he (the ruler) leads a simple life and thus sets himself as an example, he can never expect his subject to live a frugal life.

Frugal is not just about visible things. One needs to be 'frugal' in words as well. There is no need for bombastic language or impossible promises just to impress the people.

What is double virtue? We come across people who are gentle, mild and soft-spoken. But that is no indication that they have come out of temptations of five sense-organs, the desires. We also come across people who may not crave for satisfying sense organs but nevertheless, are very vindictive and wait for a chance to attack (either physically or verbally) people who have cheated them or hurt them in some way.

A man who has 'reached the Kingdom', who has achieved 'the invisible height', has reached there because he could overcome every temptation (temptations can be both positive and negative...wanting more luxuries may be termed as positive temptation while wanting to hit back or taking revenge is negative temptation). He overcomes everything because he has double Virtue.

Virtue inside ...virtue outside...the complete Tao-like person.

"This is the way to be deep rooted...."

To develop double virtue, the parents must mould their children when still young. Teaching them to forgive is also to be considered a part of spiritual moulding. But before moulding them, the parents must first live in accordance with the principles they want their children to imbibe from them. A big tree with weak roots will fall off. A grown up person without strong roots (virtue) will also fall off into undesirable activities. So let us grow deep roots of spirituality in ourselves. Then we can inspire our children by our own being. Putting our children on right track is also a divine duty towards our Creator.

60th Verse

DEVELOPING IMMUNITY

Ruling a big kingdom is like cooking a small fish.
When a man of Tao reigns over the world,
demons have no spiritual powers.
Not that the demons have no spiritual powers,
but the spirits themselves do no harm to men.
Not that the spirits do no harm to men,
but the Sage himself does no harm to his people.
If only the ruler and his people would refrain from
harming each other,
all the benefits of life would accumulate in the
kingdom.

Ruling a small country is much easier and simpler. But Lao Tzu says that when you are deeply connected to Tao, ruling even big country is like cooking a small fish.... effortless and simple, yet nourishing and all-sustaining. Not just that, small fish is easily available too! Small fish is also indicative of living a simple lifestyle.

We live in a dichotomous world. Here, all pairs of opposites exist. As said in an earlier chapter, it is like the obverse and reverse of a coin..existing together simultaneously.

When a man of Tao rules the world, demons will not trouble the inhabitants of the world.

Does it mean there will be no evil forces? To this question, the master says that though they also exist, they would have no power to trouble the people.

We all know about electrical energy, magnetic energy, hydraulic energy, atomic energy, etc. Most of us have not understood the energy of 'feelings'. As discussed in the previous passages, hate generates hate, and love generates love. This is the secret of Lord Buddha's living unharmed even while surrounded by wild animals.

If the world has Buddhas everywhere, how can there be any power to the evil forces?

Scientists have experimented with emotions on plants, which are supposed to be in the lower rung of evolutionary ladder. They have proved that plants react to our emotions.

When even plants react to emotions, how much, we humans will be impacted by others' emotions?

A sandalwood forest will have snakes too. Saints also have people in their life who dislike them and try to ruin them. Krishna's uncle wanted to kill him and sent some demons to kill the infant Krishna. But who can harm the Almighty? Did not Jesus resurrect and rise from His cross?

The great souls not only forgave their enemies, they even blessed them!! Lord Krishna gave liberation to many demons who tried to kill Him. Angulimal, who wanted to kill Lord Buddha became his disciple, overwhelmed by the love showered on him. Even in recent times, such a personality lived amongst us. Two days prior to his assassination, on 28.01.1948, Mahatma Gandhi, Father of the Indian Nation said as follows: "If I am to die by the bullet of a mad man, I must do so smiling. There must be no anger within me. God must be in my heart and on my lips". After Nathuram Godse's bullet pierced his body, he uttered the name of God, "Hey Ram"!! This reveals that he was willing to forgive even those who wanted to kill him.

Lao Tzu also speaks about 'evil spirits' from the spirit world. (the world of the dead).

Many religions follow rituals to appease their departed ancestors in different ways. It is believed that calamities will befall the family if they do not propitiate their ancestors.

Lord Krishna says thus in Bhagvad Gita:(chapter 16... shlokas 7,8,9)

Shloka 7: The person of Asurika nature (evil natured) know not what to do and what to refrain from; neither is purity found in them nor good conduct, nor truth.

Shloka 8: They say, "The universe is without truth, without a (moral) basis without god, brought about by mutual union, with lust for its cause..."

Shloka 9: Holding this view these ruined souls of small intellect and fierce deeds, rise as the enemies of the world for its destruction.

This answers many questions that go unasked out of fear, or ignorance or sheer apathy.

Let all encompassing love be our only weapon. Wars can kill so called enemies. But love kills enmity without killing enemies and gives birth to Divinity.

61st Verse

BE LIKE THE OCEAN

A great country is like the low land toward which
all streams flow.
It is the Reservoir of all under heaven, the Feminine
of the world.

The Feminine always conquers the Masculine by her
quietness,
by lowering herself through her quietness.
Hence, if a great country can lower before a small
country,
it will win over the small country;
and if small country can lower itself before a great
country,
it will win over the great country.
The one wins by stooping ;
the other by remaining low.

What a great country wants is simply to embrace more people;
and what a small country wants is simply to come to serve its patron.
Thus each gets what it wants.
But it behaves like a great country to lower itself.

History is replete with kings trying to conquer kingdoms which are small and less-powerful. Lao Tzu is comparing a great country to a female and a small country to a male. In creation, it is mostly the females that look after the young ones. In humans, it is mostly the females who run the home, look after the children, become a nurse when somebody falls ill ...a multi-faceted, multi-tasking persona....salute to them!

A mild-mannered man is teased of being 'effeminate'. Look closely into such persons, we sure will find great compassion which is many times lacking in males.

Small countries, small either in their size, resources or power, always fear powerful countries. As their power is much less than others, they take to deadly practices of planting land mines or other such devastating practices to protect themselves from other big countries.

Lao Tzu guides bigger and powerful countries to come forward by extending their hands in friendship. The less powerful country, setting aside unnecessary ego conflicts, if it reciprocates the friendship, both big and small countries will be benefitted. Lao Tzu is describing big country as female and small country as male. His presentation of ideal world is very revolutionary. Usually, big is associated with male and small with females.

urt   ay

The genius that he is, he is comparing the powerful countries as females. In creation, it is always the male which is very dominant; it has to be aggressive to win over the female species. The females just receives the males and are many times passive.

When a powerful nation rooted in Tao embraces the smaller nations, there will be no trace of any fear of power. Absence of fear will make the small nations to willingly accept the bigger nations as a small child leans on to his mother. Thus both thrive on each other without striving.

62nd Verse

THE ONLY REFUGE

The Tao is the hidden Reservoir of all things.
A treasure to the honest, it is a safeguard to the erring.

A good word will find its own market.
A good deed may be used as a gift to another.
That a man is straying from the right path
is no reason that he should be cast away.

Hence, as the Enthronement of an Emperor,
Or at the installation of the Three Ministers,
let others offer their discs of jade,
following it up with teams of horses;
it is better for you to offer the Tao without moving
your feet!

Why did the ancients prize the Tao?
Is it not because by virtue of it he who seeks finds,
And the guilty are forgiven?
That is why it is such a treasure to the world.

**The Tao is the hidden Reservoir of all things.
A treasure to the honest, it is a safeguard to the erring.**

Tao is all-encompassing. The simplest way to express this idea is to compare it to the sky which is all encompassing. The honest and the dishonest, the saint and the sinner, the rich and the poor, the visible and the invisible are all covered by sky or space.

The erring children are easily forgiven by their parents. Adi Shankaracharya extols motherhood by saying *"kuputraha jayathe kadachith...kumatha na bhavathi..."* there can be bad children...but never a bad mother. *Shakthi* worship or worshipping the female aspect of God is preferred by many, as in such a form of worship, the devotee feels emotionally more close to the Mother. *Navarathri* festival held during the month of September or October is dedicated to Goddesses *Durga, Lakshmi and Saraswati* (three days to each deity, in the order given). The last day or tenth day is *Vijayadashami* or Victory Day.

A good deed may be used as a gift to another.

In India, before any important function, it is customary to touch the feet of the elders to seek their blessings. Many families still follow this beautiful tradition. Blessings are invisible. Invisible things will never cease to be. Blessings arise from loving thoughts. It costs nothing. It needs nothing. No time or space has any constraint on it. It needs only purity of thought and word. Let us lavish blessings on others.

A good word will find its own market.
A good deed may be used as a gift to another.
That a man is straying from the right path
is no reason that he should be cast away.

Hence, as the Enthronement of an Emperor,
Or at the installation of the Three Ministers,
let others offer their discs of jade,
following it up with teams of horses;
it is better for you to offer the Tao without moving
your feet!
Why did the ancients prize the Tao?
Is it not because by virtue of it he who seeks finds,
And the guilty are forgiven?
That is why it is such a treasure to the world.

Buying and selling of goods is the main activity in any market. The 'product' Lao Tzu is offering for sale are his 'good words'. Is it not a rare commodity nowadays? Sellers are few, but there are many buyers as 'good words' are a tonic to our suffering souls.

A saint poet of Maharashtra says "I sell God's name".

that a man is straying from the right path
is no reason that he should be cast away.

Have we not made mistakes in our lives? We all have our dark side. If we have to cast away a man for his mistakes, we may have to cast ourselves away first!

Let me recall the story of how Jesus protected the so-called fallen woman. It seems that there was a woman who was accused of being unfaithful to her husband. She was accused of having a love affair with another man. A mob had gathered while the husband was shouting at the woman and beating her. Soon, the mob was also mercilessly throwing stones at her. Jesus rushed there to protect the helpless woman. He stood shielding the woman and asked her husband to forgive her mistake. Jesus then told the mob, "Only the one who has never committed a sin in his mind can punish a sinner". The mob realized their mistake. They left the scene with their heads hung low, as they realized that they too had fallen prey to their own desires in their own minds.

The guilty are forgiven...

Criminals need compassion. Their inner sickness comes out in the form of criminal activities. Most of them belong to broken families. Like a rudderless boat, they are swayed by the waves of passion and lose their way.

There is so much of baggage behind a criminal. A balloon inflated beyond its capacity breaks with a small little pin prick. The law-breakers are just like the balloon - the pin is the visible man (the so-called criminal) and the inflated balloon is his unhappy background. Nobody becomes a criminal overnight. Poverty, neglect, lack of education, unhappy homes are some of the reasons for people to get into nefarious activities. Imagine an innocent child spending his beautiful childhood amidst such surroundings. Thus we see criminal is 'made' and not 'born'.

He is almost driven to undesirable activities and over a period of time he stands before the society as a criminal.

A man immersed in Tao, will see beyond the criminal. Just casting away the 'pin pricked balloon', is not going to solve any problem. Behind a criminal are many invisible entities in the form of people at home, his surroundings, friends, etc. If such is the case, why to punish just one? As parents play a very great role, it becomes our divine duty to live a harmonious living for our children to grow as an emotionally balanced people. Charity begins at home is the best way to express this idea.

Ordinary persons are not able to see beyond 'one person', the criminal. Tao knows the back ground. That is why he says 'guilty are forgiven'. To help a person to come out of his negativity is as holy a task as constructing hospitals or temples. It is considered a very sacred duty to construct temples. Preserving and looking after the already existing temples are equally important. According to Hinduism, every man and woman has the potential to raise to the level of godhead. In other words we are god potential. Is it not our duty to look after them as much as we can?

63rd Verse

ATTITUDE TOWARDS LIFE

Do the Non- Ado.
Strive for the effortless.
Savour the savourless.
Exalt the low.
Multiply the few.
Requite injury with kindness.

Nip troubles in the bud.
Sow the great in the small.

Difficult things of the world can only be tackled
when they are easy.
Big things of the world can only be achieved by
attending to their small beginnings.
Thus, the Sage never has to grapple with big things,
Yet he alone is capable of achieving them!

He who promises lightly must be lacking in faith.
He who thinks everything easy will end by finding
everything difficult.
Therefore, the Sage who regards everything as
difficult,
meets with no difficulties in the end.

What effort do we make when we sleep for the breath to flow, and the body to grow? All our external activities take rest when we sleep. In deep sleep we know nothing and do nothing. Then, how do we breathe when we are fast asleep? Who is the doer? Does he (doer) come only when I sleep to keep me breathing or is he always present? Something is constantly working all through our lives, even when we are asleep.

Without any ado, every organ is functioning when we sleep. In fact, during sleep, our body rejuvenates itself for the next day. People with lack of sleep feel and look sick. People in great physical or emotional pain are given sedatives so that they get some sleep. In fact, many types of sickness are because of lack of proper sleep.

A man of Tao functions like the breathing process during sleep. Effortless, yet all the vital functions of the body do their job which is necessary for our effort (functioning).

It is much simpler to be kind hearted, generous, and forgiving than to speak truth always. Let us think of it...even dyeing white hair to look younger is a form of lie! I cheat myself by doing so. Cheating others is different...but when somebody cheats himself, that is stupidity.

savour the savourless.

Lao Tzu may not be referring to food alone. Some religions advocate bland food on certain days or months, so that we overcome our addiction to taste.

During illness, our health care professionals and doctors advise us on foods to be avoided and foods to be taken. Food plays a major role in our life. Whether we observe food restrictions in our life because of our religious beliefs or because of our health awareness is a different question.

We like people praising us. But when somebody criticizes us, we do not like them. "Leaving behind a sour taste in the mouth" aptly describes in physical terms our condition or reaction to words of criticism.

Even if we do not protest outwardly to criticisms, our body does react to such comments as we have not lifted ourselves up from the influence of 'good and bad' behavior of others.

A man of Tao, like the sky is unaffected by others' views and opinions, as he is firmly rooted in his own self. He is a *sthitapragna*.

Exalt the low

Compassion need not surface only when somebody is in pain. People develop inferiority complex for various reasons like lack of education, physical features, poverty or any other reason. They many times hide themselves and thus their chance of blossoming into a beautiful human is unfortunately and unnecessarily lost.

Swami Vivekananda used to say; 'each man is potentially divine'. How to bring out the inherent divinity? There are as many ways as the number of people, for each one has to work out his karma according to his own nature.

Lao Tzu is asking us to 'exalt the low'. Dr. Ambedkar of India worked tirelessly for the down trodden and socially ostracized people. Martin Luther King is another example of "exalt the low" for he worked for the black people and brought dignity into their lives. Dignity is another quality of divinity.

Multiply the few:

People who are committed to others' welfare without having an axe to grind, are, unfortunately only a handful. The world we live in at present need more such selfless people. When there is an inner awakening to do our little bit, we will join these 'few' and thus help in increasing their number.

sow the great in the small;

When we "exalt the low" and "multiply the few", we are "sowing" the great (the inherent Godliness) in the small (people who are apparently low spiritually ...but potentially high). My guru encouraged us to chant "soham" (saha aham)...which means "I AM THAT". With this repeated chanting, some profound but inexplicable and invisible changes take place within that person. This has to be experienced, and it cannot be explained in words.

requite injury with kindness:

Thiruvalluvar, A sage poet from Tamil Nadu says in his Thirukkural (holy sound or voice) Innasaidarai otrudal avar nana nannayam saiduvidal ....(verse no. 314) which means... (counter the person who hurt you by being good or doing good to him.)

Even taking revenge can be made holy, when there is an understanding of the principle of **oneness** beyond the apparent multitudes.

When a man goes to a doctor when his condition becomes hopeless, the doctor says: 'you should have come earlier'. 'Nipping in the bud' is very important. Before a catastrophe strikes, let us take steps to avoid future escalation of problems.

Nobody becomes a thief or a terrorist overnight. If people at home are vigilant about any member of their family going astray, they should spare no effort to bring them back with love and care avoiding unpleasant, hurtful language.

A man of Tao will take care of even small details when undertaking a project. We all know how a war was lost because of a 'horse shoe'.

Let us not forget that every nut and bolt in its correct place makes the big machinery function properly. Can we afford to be negligent?

A small seed is behind the huge tree. It is important that the seed is taken care of properly so that it grows into a tree.

Sky-scrapers are also built step by step and each step involves many steps.

64th Verse

TIMELY ACTION

What is at rest is easy to hold.
What manifests no omens is easily forestalled.
What is fragile is easily shattered.
What is small is easily scattered.

Tackle things before they have appeared.
Cultivate peace and order before confusion and disorder have set in.
A tree as big as a man's embrace springs from a tiny sprout.
A tower nine story height begins with a heap of earth.
A journey of a thousand leagues starts from where your feet stand.

He who fusses over anything spoils it.
He who grasps anything loses it.
The Sage fusses over nothing and therefore spoils nothing.
He grips at nothing and therefore loses nothing.

In handling affairs, people often spoil them just at the point of success.
With heedfulness in the beginning and patience at the end nothing will be spoiled.
Therefore, the Sage desires to be desireless,
Sets no value on rare goods,
Learns to unlearn his learning,
And induces the masses to return from where they have overpassed.
He only helps all creatures to find their own nature,
But does not venture to lead them by the nose.

---

what is at rest is easy to hold.
what manifests no omens is easily forestalled.
what is fragile is easily shattered.
what is small is easily scattered.

It is easy to control an animal when it is resting. Once it is on its feet, it will become difficult to restrain it. Similarly, children can easily be moulded. It is up to the parents to guide their children into being loving and caring humans. It is very unfortunate that people recruit children to take up deadly arms in the name of religion or some perverted ideology. Let us do our best to put off fire before it bursts as a huge conflagration. To make it simple to understand - "a stitch in time saves nine."

We can take care for our health by taking preventative measures which are in the form of vaccines. Thus, we protect ourselves against many types of diseases. We know that 'prevention is better than cure'. Many countries have been successful in eradicating deadly diseases like polio, and small pox by regular vaccination.

Anger and hatred are diseases of the mind. All of us, irrespective of what religion we belong to, or which country we belong to, are responsible to mould our future generation towards goodwill for all...and hatred towards none.

"Boond boond paani sagar ko bhar deta hai" says a Hindi poet. It means every drop of water constitutes an ocean. Nothing is insignificant...not even a drop of water.

Even a little effort from us can bring about such a heaven on earth.

The journey towards this direction may be long....

But let us remember the master's words...

a journey of a thousand leagues starts from where your feet stands.

It is human weakness to impose one's ideas on people around them. This self-righteous attitude make others shun such a person..

As opposed to this, is a man of Tao. He neither preaches nor gives sermons standing on a high pedestal. He lives such a life that people start emulating him. This is how he 'teaches without teaching' and 'does everything by doing nothing'. There is no personal agenda behind any of his actions.

What is the secret behind such detachment to worldly things?

Thiruvalluvar says: "pattruga patratran patrinai; appatrinai patruga patruvidarku" which means "Desire the desire of desireless God ..so that desire ceases to desire......"

A man of Tao leans on the Source of 10,000 things (God) and It's wisdom. His surrender to the Supreme makes whatever he does as an offering to the Almighty.

does not lead them by nose ...

Bulls have rope running through their nostrils. Its owner drags the animal, whether it wants to go nor not. The bull has no free will.

We also know the story of donkey being led by a carrot dangling in the front. Its nose smells the carrot, eyes see it, its tongue desires it. It makes vain attempts to get grip of it. The carrot is just a bait for the donkey to move forward.

Working with a true master is a sacred freedom for his aura is such that a person melts like snow in his divine warmth.

He will never put a noose on our nose nor will he dangle a carrot (temptation of going to heaven...or any other benefit). In fact, a true master like Lao Tzu have come to disentangle us from the invisible noose (in the form of attachment to worldly objects) and lead us to spiritual freedom called liberation.

Whether a spiritual organization or a corporate office, the three 'Ms' play the main role.

'Men' (also women)...Money and Material. Of the three, the first, that is 'men' (and women) have to be handled with care and concern. Without them, the money and material that is put in will be useless.

65th Verse

BE THE SYMBOL OF SIMPLICITY

In the old days, those who were well versed in the practice of the Tao did not try to enlighten the people, but rather to keep them in the state of simplicity.

For, why are the people hard to govern?

Because they are too clever!

Therefore, he who governs his state with cleverness is its malefactor;

but he who governs his state without resorting to cleverness is its benefactor.

To know these principles is to possess a rule and a measure.

To keep the rule and the measure constantly in your mind is what we call mystical virtue.

Deep and far reaching is Mystical Virtue!

It leads all things to return, till they come back to Great Harmony.

Hinduism describes the four Ages of the world. 1. Satya yuga. 2.Threta yuga..3.Dwapar yuga and 4.Kali yuga.(each yuga, that is Age consists of lakhs of years).

The yugas are compared by using the example of a cow.

1. In the satya yuga, the yuga of truth (total Godliness) the cow stands firm on four legs. There is supreme peace and everyone is living in bliss.

2. In the Threta yuga, the cow is standing on three legs. It means, some instability has crept in.

3.In Dwapar yuga, the cow has only two legs now. It is very unstable and faltering at every step.

4. In Kali yuga the cow has only one leg left. It is totally helpless. It is bleeding and pleading for help. According to Hindu mythology, we are living at present in 'kali yuga'.

In Satya yuga, there was just God and Godliness. According to me, Lao Tzu describes such a state as 'primal virtue". As everything was divine, there were no rules and regulations. Neither was there any need for teachers or gurus nor for rituals to be followed.

The subsequent yugas slowly lost their 'primal simplicity' and that led to 'governance'. Cunning and powerful people started ruling over others. Simplicity was simply lost and complexity took over the lives of people. Money and power became synonymous. At times, they were traded. Money gave power and power gave money.

Cleverness many times hides cunningness. Cunning people will encounter more of their own kind and the struggle for supremacy will raise its ugly heads everywhere.

When the ruler is deeply rooted in Tao, he will rule without 'ruling over'. Such a person is said to posses 'mystical virtue'. To get back our 'mystical virtue', we have to re-trace our step. To live in peace, we have to go back and find out from where we came from and where we shall be going. We have to work on ourselves. May patience and perseverance become our foundation so that we reach Home.

66th Verse

LOSER IS THE WINNER

How does the sea become the king of all streams?
Because it lies lower than they!
Hence it is king of all streams.

Therefore, the Sage reigns over the people by
humbling himself by speech;
And leads the people by putting himself behind.

Thus it is that when a Sage stands above the people,
they do not feel the heaviness of his weight;
And when he stands in front of the people, they do
not feel hurt.

Therefore all the world is glad to push him forward
without getting tired of him.
Just because he strives with nobody, nobody can ever
strive with him.

The height of a land is measured with reference to sea level, even if there is no sea in that particular region or area. The rivers have their origin in a mountain or a hill. The gravitational pull brings them down and somehow they find their way to sea. This again is a metaphor ...a sage is like a sea...at the lowest level by humbling himself and the rivers are the people who want to know the meaning of life.

A man of Tao does not brag about his achievements or knowledge....and there is no need to, for his actions speak louder than words. As there is no need to prove himself, he does not indulge in 'one-upmanship' or get into any unpleasant show of power or knowledge.

We either develop inferiority complex or hatred when people want to show that they have something special... something which no body has. Religious fanatics want to 'prove' that their 'religion' is the only way and all other religions are false religions.

I have had the greatest good fortune of being with enlightened masters. What Lao Tzu is describing about saintly people has to be experienced. Again I consider myself as very fortunate to be associated with such masters. I understood the real meaning of the word "humility". The problem between man and his own inherent divinity is his ego. When it dissolves, divinity shines in all its glory.

Egoless person has nothing to prove - either about his knowledge or the ignorance of others. He does not interfere with other's belief system. Like a gardener, he allows the plant to grow by creating a loving atmosphere. He allows a rose to be a rose. He understands that a rose can never be a lotus. Both belong to the Creator. A true master is just a facilitator and that is the end of his job.

Every religion is a special flower at the feet of the Creator. Let us respect the variety.

Lao Tzu has given us a new definition of 'leadership'. This 'leadership' is not about 'doing' but 'being'. When the false facade of superiority is dropped, we move away from 'doing' and go closer to 'being'.

67th Verse

THE HOLY TRINITY

All the world says that my Tao is great,
but seems queer, like nothing on earth.
But it is just because my Tao is great it is like nothing
on earth!
If it were like anything on earth, how small it would
have been from the very beginning!

I have Three Treasures, which I hold fast and watch
over closely.
The first is Mercy;
the second is Frugality.
The third is Not Daring to be first in the world.
Because I am merciful, therefore I can be brave.
Because I am frugal, therefore I can be generous.
Because I dare not be first, therefore I can be the
chief of all vessels.

If a man wants to be brave without first being merciful,
generous without first being frugal,
a leader without first wishing to follow,
he is only courting death!

Mercy alone can help you to win a war.
Mercy alone can help you to defend your state.
For Heaven will come to the rescue of the merciful,
and protect him with *it's* Mercy.

We describe God as 'Ocean of Mercy' 'Ocean of Love' etc. Ocean is just a small part of this earth and earth itself is just a speck in this cosmos. Thus every language falls flat while describing the glory of the Almighty. There is no way to describe the Supreme Power. When we pray to God for wealth or health, or promotion (or any favors that we seek), it means we value them (the favors that we seek) more than God.God becomes second fiddle.

A minimum of two things are needed for comparison. When there is comparison, we tend to take sides as per our understanding and our personal yard-sticks.

We compare even air as being warm, hot or cold though air can never be divided. This comparison arises because of location and other factors.

We say the sky is overcast. We make such statement in spite of knowing that sky is 'nothing' or a non-thing. Words and expressions are limited and to describe the indescribable like God is impossible. Hence, we attribute all good qualities to God, like He is Mercy, Love, Compassion, Abundance and what not.

Things on earth and from earth have beginning and an end. In between these two phases living things have growth.

I have Three Treasures, which I hold fast and watch over closely.
The first is *Mercy*;
the second is *Frugality*.
The third is *Not Daring to be first in the world*.
Because I am merciful, therefore I can be brave.
Because I am frugal, therefore I can be generous.
Because I dare not be first, therefore I can be the chief of all vessels.

If a man wants to be brave without first being merciful,
generous without first being frugal,
a leader without first wishing to follow,
he is only courting death!

Mercy alone can help you to win a war.
mercy alone can help you to defend your state.
for heaven will come to the rescue of the merciful,
and protect him with Its Mercy.

Every religion says "God is mercy, God is love". Is it not our duty towards the religion we belong to, to put these words into action? Let us ponder over it.

Lao Tzu says "I have three treasures". Whatever we consider to be our treasure, we will safeguard it under any circumstances. The master's three treasures are:

the first is mercy;
because I am merciful, therefore I can be brave.
mercy alone can help you to win a war.
for heaven will come to the rescue of the merciful,
and protect him with Its Mercy.
mercy alone can help you to defend your state.

Can we be merciful in war?

A man like Lao Tzu is merciful while waging a war. Even if he wields a sword, it will be to protect his people from enemies and as such there is no hatred. When a wild animal attacks us, we use weapons to protect ourselves. There is no enmity towards animals.

Why do wild animals attack humans? We have indiscriminately destroyed their forests. Otherwise there is enough food for every animal, whether carnivorous or herbivorous. Many carnivorous animals do not kill unless hungry.

People run away when they have to confront unpleasant situation. There is verbal war and emotional war as well. There is a saying in Tamil language "theeyai anaipadu thee alla…oru theemaikku theemai marundalla…theeyai thanneer anaituvidum…saida theemayai nanmai thiruthividum." It means that fire is not put out by fire…antidote for injury in not another injury…fire is put out by water…injury is healed by goodness.(the word injury here has many dimensions… physical injury, emotional injury, cheating, slandering etc.)

Emperor Ashoka was heartbroken to see the devastation brought about in the Kalinga war. He gave up everything and became a monk.

Even in the hearts of hard core criminals, there shines the spark of divinity waiting to reveal itself. Mercy and patience should be our two legs to march toward Tao. Let us develop such noble qualities.

Anger gives us the illusion of bravery. All the action movies in any language have heroes seeking revenge. They also justify their action. Let us remember what Buddha had said "anger destroys us first...before it destroys others."

for heaven will come to the rescue of the merciful, and protect him with Its Mercy.

A Sankrit verse says: *dharmo rakshati rakshitaha*...one who protects or upholds virtue...Virtue (God or Tao) will uphold him (protect him).

the second is frugality
generous without first being frugal,

Austerity is the true hall-mark of a sage. He does not hoard things nor hold on to them. His needs are simple... his language is simple...his living is simple. Because of such attitude, there is no shortage of anything in his life. He joyously shares his abundance with others. A man requested Jesus to accept him as his disciple. Jesus said: "Go and distribute everything". The man hung his head down and went away, as he was not willing to let go of his property.

the third is Not Daring to be first in the world

Jesus says: "one who stands last, stands first.".

Standing first has to be understood in a deeper sense. What makes us wanting all the time to stand first?

Let us consider some basic instincts which push us towards being 'first' always:

1) Fear- People jump queues out of fear of not being able to get what they have been waiting for.
2) Insecurity - People want to make themselves visible especially in a social or political gathering so that they get noticed by others.
3) Pride - To prove their own worth...(whatever it might be)
4) Ego – it is another word for pride..

Whenever there is any competition, people wish him "come first". We can re-phrase it by saying; "do your best... very best...and forget the rest (results)".

68ᵗʰ Verse

DIVINE WEDDING

A good soldier is never aggressive;
A good fighter is never angry.
The best way of conquering an enemy is to win him over by not
antagonizing him.
The best way of employing a man is to serve under him.
This is called the virtue of non striving!
This is called using the abilities of men!
This is called being wedded to heaven as of old!

Somebody asked Satya Sai Baba of India: "Are you a Guru? Are you an *Avatar* (incarnation), are you a Messenger?"

Baba said : "I am a servant"

When I first read this message in one of the books on Baba, I was aghast. (Baba is also lovingly addressed as Swami by His devotees). I pondered over this statement. It brought tears to my eyes. Yes, God is used by many of us as a servant. "Do this for me"... that for me... this for my son…. this for my husband…the list is endless. I confess I used my so-called devotion as a tool to get what I desired. Forgive me Swami!

We are constantly engaged in doing different things for our family. Do I go and tell my neighbor that I bought a saree for my mother or a mobile for my father? We do everything out of love for our family members. But when we do for the society, we want the print and the electronic media to cover the event. Seeking publicity is another incurable disease of the society.

What is being wedded to heaven? Heaven is another way of referring to Almighty.

In Indian culture, wedding is not just another event in life. It is being with each other till the body drops dead. They support each other, nourish each other and work together.

A tiger has a tigress as his partner,..a lion has a lioness as his partner.

A person is wedded to God if he develops Godly qualities as described in the previous chapters. As Tao is neither male nor female, our gender also will make no difference in divine wedding. If such a divine union takes place, that is the heaven on earth. All of us are given a chance to marry God. Let us come out our small little frame of males and females and prepare ourselves to be God's consort. That is probably the reason why, in Indian or Hindu Philosophy, the Primordial being is considered as the only male, while all other beings, (irrespective of being male or female) are considered females in front of God.

69th Verse

VICTORY IS DEATH-KNELL

The strategists have a saying : I dare not be a host
but rather a guest;
I dare not advance an inch but rather retreat a foot.
This is called marching without moving,
Rolling up one's sleeves without baring one's arms,
Capturing the enemy without confronting him,
Holding a weapon that is invisible.
There is no greater calamity than to under-estimate
the strength of your enemy.
For to under- estimate the strength of your enemy is
to lose your treasure.
Therefore when opposing troops meet in battle,
victory belongs to the grieving side.

Lao Tzu's advocates peace under all circumstances
which includes a violent place like battle field as well. We
should not leave any stone unturned to live in peace and
harmony.

Our not being interested in waging wars is not going to stop others from attacking us. When such a situation develops, where the war becomes inevitable, a wise man will never underestimate his enemies. Keeping ourselves in readiness is the intelligent way to face wars or war-like situation. War is a team-work of hundreds and thousands of people. A mule carrying food or arms supply is equally important. Anything important has to be looked after properly. To look after them properly, one has to take guidance and help from others. Thinking, planning and executing the duty properly and on time is also a strategy of war. Physical and financial conditions, strategies to be adopted, weather conditions, the terrain and other relevant details are also to be considered and worked out before entering into a battle-field.

In war, both the parties face terrible, irrevocable loss of lives and property. The lives that are lost leave behind hundreds and thousands family members whose lives will never be the same again. The victor also mourns the death of soldiers and other people killed in war. Beneath the glory of victory lay dead the gory aftermath of war.

Ironically, the victorious side has more people killed than the side which is defeated. The burning desire to win a war, makes a king recruit more people and train them in every possible strategy. War in those days depended mainly on the strength (the number) of soldiers. Indirectly, winning a war means losing your dear citizens.

70ᵗʰ Verse

SAINT IS A CHANNEL

My words are very easy to understand and very easy
to practice:
but the world cannot understand them nor practice
them.

My words have an Ancestor.
My deeds have a Lord.
The people have no knowledge of this.
Therefore, they have no knowledge of me.

The fewer persons know me,
the nobler are they that follow me.
Therefore, the Sage wears coarse clothes,
while keeping jade in his bosom.

Lao Tzu never seems to tire of using paradoxes to put
forward his ideas.

He says: **"My words are very easy to understand and very easy to practice."**

in the very next sentence he says:

"but the world cannot understand them nor practice them."

What are his words?

1) Live in this world like a guest...it is a temporary abode.
2) Avoid wars...(that includes verbal wars which over a period of time snow-balls into physical wars.)
3) Live in harmony with nature.
4) Your presence should not disturb others...live in such obscurity.
5) Lead a frugal life ...when you have less, where is no fear of losing?
6) The Supreme Power or Tao is all encompassing...it does not belong to any religion.
7) Rituals are like a child learning through simple games. Once you learn (understand) the Supreme Power behind everything, rituals automatically drop.

How simple are the messages given by the Master! If we understand these simple truths and put them in practice, we will have heaven on earth.

Why is it difficult to follow the path of noble balance advocated by Lao Tzu?

The reason is people have become self-centered, egoistic, and narrow minded and the holy books are in wrong hands. Nobody can deny the destruction caused by war. In spite of knowing that even victory is going to bring grief to many families, there seems no end to war-mongering.

Lao Tzu says;
"My words have an ancestor".

The ancestral property I own now is not because of much effort from my side. It has been handed down to me. This is the meaning of "my words have an ancestor".

The incarnation of humility that Lao Tzu is, he does not even want to take credit of such wisdom which he is showering upon people who care to listen to him.

A true saint will not try to show off his knowledge of power. He knows he is not the owner the messages that he is giving us. When you own a Mercedes Benz car, you like to show it off. When you hire a Mercedes Benz, as you are not the owner, you do not bother to show off, because you do not own it.

A true saint has no ownership...either of material possession or his spiritual wisdom.

71st Verse

SECRET OF HEALTH

To realize that our knowledge is ignorance,
this is a noble insight.
To regard our ignorance as knowledge,
this is mental sickness.

Only when we are sick of our sickness,
shall we cease to be sick.
The Sage is not sick, being sick of sickness;
this is the secret of health.

What ails or troubles the world right now?

Religion, which is supposed to uplift us, unite us, and lead us towards harmony and love of Almighty, seems to be a major sickness the world is suffering from now.

Why is this sickness created in the name of God? The main reason is incorrect understanding and interpretation about the messages contained in the holy books of all religions. The half-baked knowledge about religion is killing not just humans but also humanity. Pray, tell me, which God that you worship will be happy to see His creation being destroyed ruthlessly? How will you account for the death of children born in some religion but adopted and raised by people of other religion?

A man who knows nothing about the messages contained in holy books but prays to the Supreme power in his own child-like simplicity will be the most precious gift to the world. His simplicity is such that there is no fear, hatred or ill-will towards others.

Let us become such a precious 'gift' and lift up others who need our help.

Religious fanatics are using their knowledge of science and technology for destroying people of other faith. In fact, many of them are highly qualified people. Smartly dressed, they seldom reveal the poison inside their hearts. Behind that veil, is the person full of wrong understanding of his holy book. Their appearances hide their heart full of hatred towards other religions and fear of losing their identity. The volcano in them is always simmering.

Every religion wants to crush the people of other faiths. The demoralized demons demolish dignity and divinity of the religion they are supposed to profess.

We can cure ourselves only when we realize that:-

1) We have caused the sickness.
2) We can also cure it.

As no criminal wants to admit he is a criminal, no religion wants to come forward and accept their own destructive nature which is the outcome of incorrect understanding of Almighty. The step towards the cure is to first realize that we are sick.

72nd Verse

GIVING SAFETY IS SAINTLY

When the people no longer fear your power,
it is a sign that a greater power is coming.

Interfere not lightly with their dwelling
nor lay heavy burdens upon their livelihood.
Only when you cease to weary them,
they will cease wearied of you.

Therefore the sage knows himself,
but makes no show of himself.
Laughs himself,
but does not exalt himself.
He prefers what is within to what is without.

Many times, a person in power creates fear to show off
his supremacy. People pretend to respect him but behind his
back, hate him and wait for a chance to topple and trample
upon him. A man immersed in Tao will never display his

power or position. He understands and empathizes with others and will not burden them with unnecessary taxes and other financial burdens. When a person is over-taxed he will try every possible means to avoid it. Crooks are born as tax-evaders.

Another paradox of life is that when we do not show off our power (in spite of our having it), more power seems to enter our energy field. Only a humble person can achieve this sort of attitude. This is egolessness. Egolessness is called emptiness. Nature never allows emptiness. Thus a man of Tao goes on receiving more and more power. There is a saying in India: "When you know yourself, you know everything that is to be known". What do I know about myself?...that I am so and so, living in such and such place...what else do I know about myself? Who am I? Where did I come from? Where will I go? I know nothing. In fact only seers know about such truth about themselves and also others. In spite of knowing, they will not embarrass us by disclosing all details about our private lives. Let us compare ourselves with these holy people. We brand people. "Oh! That man! I know him well...he is such a crook!" Before knowing the 'crook', he has to know himself. If he succeeds in this, he will realize the same divinity running through every atom in this cosmos. With this wisdom in his bosom, he can only laugh, because most of the people who go to him carry with them their bundle of karmas and expect somebody to unburden them.

Lao Tzu says; "Laughs himself".....to know the truth and yet not embarrass others by revealing it is one of the greatest virtue.

73ʳᵈ Verse

HIS WILL PREVAILS

He who is brave in daring will be killed;
he who is brave in not daring will survive.
Of these two kinds of bravery, one is beneficial,
while the other proves harmful.
Some things are detested by Heaven, but who knows
the reason?
Even the Sage is baffled by such a question.

It is Heaven's way to conquer without striving,
to get responses without speaking,
to induce the people to come without summoning,
to act according to plans without haste.

Vast is Heaven's nest;
Sparse—meshed it is, and yet,
Nothing can slip through it.

What is bravery? A person holding a weapon or going to war is supposed to be brave. Can 'killing' be termed as bravery? According to Lao Tzu, a person with inner strength is truly brave. This inner strength will not allow him to wield a weapon unnecessarily. But a man without this inner strength will carry a gun and go to war at the drop of a hat.

Arjun, our hero from Mahabharat also did not want to go to war. His reluctance was not based on understanding but was based on his own strong feelings and attachment towards his opponents who were his close family people.

Krishna chides this by saying: *'anarya'*:...you are unlike an Arya. (Here, the word Arya is not a race...it is a reference made to the kingly quality of being a brave warrior).

Lao Tzu indirectly refers to theory of karma. He says: **"vast is heaven's nest; sparse –meshed it is and yet nothing can slip through it.**

Theory of karma can be understood from a scientific point of view also. It is a well-known scientific law that every action has an equal and opposite reaction.

The arrow we send will come back to us in its own time.

The sending of arrows is a physical action.

Do we not do mental action all through our lives? Yes, we do.

All deep rooted thoughts that we have, have the potential to manifest themselves in our life in due course. We know that time taken for growth and for yielding of fruits is different for different trees; so too, our karmas yield fruits (results) as per invisible Divine Law. That is why Dr. Wayne says "Change Your Thoughts, Change Your life".

74th Verse

OVERCOMING FEAR OF DEATH

When the people are no longer afraid of death,
why scare them with spectre of death?

If you could make the people always afraid of death,
and they still persisted in breaking the law,
Then you might with reason arrest and execute them,
and who would dare to break the law?

Is not the Great Executor always there to kill?
To do the killing for the Great Executor
is to chop wood for a master carpenter,
and you would be lucky indeed if you did not hurt
your own hand!

---

when the people are no longer afraid of death,
why scare them with spectre of death?

History tells us how holy people were hounded, tortured and threatened with painful death. The list is long. Jesus was crucified. Buddha was threatened with dire consequences. Saint Meera was given poison. So was Socrates.

These great people had realized the truth of life and also the truth of death. Then who could threaten them with death?

Lao Tzu is about the sanctity of life... the sanctity of lives of even criminals. He is not for punishment. Why do we have so many rules and regulations? As one man's food can be another man's poison, certain laws that prevail in a country are frowned upon by other countries. For example, marriage of same sex is accepted in some countries whereas it is frowned upon by others. Abortion is legal in some countries and forbidden by law in another. Laws are made so that people live within the accepted way of life. Does making laws stop crimes, rapes or murders?

Unfortunately the crimes rates are increasing all over the world. In some countries death sentences by stoning people to death still exists. But in spite of such a law, there does not seem to be any change in the attitude of hard core criminals who destroy lives.

According to Lao Tzu, capital punishment is not correct. As we cannot give life, we can also not take life. The Supreme Being which gives us life will decide about death as well. Who are we to kill, when we cannot give life? It is easy to pluck a flower. But nobody can put it back on the plant.

According to Indian Philosophy, the thoughts remain in the ether when a person dies. Execution of criminals, thus is no real solution to improve the condition of the world; for the persons thus executed leave behind their negative thoughts which prevail or affect and create negative people to complete the unfinished task.

Nothing is ever wasted ...neither good thought nor bad thought...In due course, they will surface again through somebody.

How, then, can we create a beautiful world for ourselves?

What is the solution then? Change your thoughts and change the world!

———◆———

75th Verse

MONSTER MONARCH

Why are the people starving?
Because those above them are taxing them too
heavily.
That is why they are starving.

Why are the people hard to manage?
Because those above them are fussy and have private
ends to serve.
That is why they are hard to manage.

Why do the people make light of death?
Because those above them make too much of life.
That is why they make light of death.

The people have simply nothing to live upon!
They know better than to value such a life!

---

why do the people make light of death?
because those above them make too much of life.
that is why they make light of death.

Murder is an unnatural way of leaving this world. So is suicide.

Lao Tzu always insists on 'natural living'. "Natural living" naturally will include "natural death" as well.

Frustration, despondency, ridicule and low self-esteem makes a person take his own life. Suicide is self-murder.

Anger and hatred makes a person take others lives. He becomes a murderer.

I was pondering over the above two unfortunate and painful souls screaming for help.

Can we not listen to them with not just ears but with our hearts as well?

Why does such a situation arise in this world where people are slaughtered mercilessly?

According to Lao Tzu violence is because of people in authority - be it in politics or religion. Executing a criminal or a murderer sounds like a strange law indeed!

You kill him because he killed somebody....Can fire put out fire? Think over it

76th Verse

RIGIDITY IS DEADLY

When a man is living he is soft and supple.
When he is dead, he becomes hard and rigid.
When a plant is living, it is soft and tender.
When it is dead, it becomes withered and dry.

Hence, the hard and rigid belongs to the company of the dead:
The soft and supple belongs to the company of the living.

Therefore, a mighty army tends to fall by it's own weight,
Just as dry wood is ready for the axe.

The mighty and great will be laid low;
The humble and week will be exalted.

The most supple is a living being in its mother's womb... whether humans or animals. In that little space called womb, it grows from a tiny cell to a full-fledged living being. If it were to be rigid, it would pierce the womb and rupture it. It will die before being born.

Suppleness is life...rigidity is death.

Rigidity based on religious belief is like the most dreaded disease called cancer. You do not know where, how, why and when it will strike.

Variety is the spice of life, somebody said. Not just nature, but even languages are in abundance in India. We have people with different religious back ground. There is great variety in the way we dress, in the way we pray and in the way we live. It follows naturally that there are different customs and traditions. Unfortunately, this variety can also lead to unnecessary divisions based on language and other factors.

Variety need not be the spice of life....it may even smell of destruction if not handled with care, keeping the larger picture in mind. Language is just another tool to open us to the vastness of creation. Let us expand ourselves.

Every religion has its own rigid ideas of worship. Anybody deviating from laid down manner of worship is frowned upon. People follow rituals only out of fear of God. It is sad that people who should be joyously singing the glory of God, get trapped into rituals out of fear and we know fear and faith cannot co-exist. Unscrupulous religious leaders frighten the gullible simple people into following rigid code of conduct in dress, marriages, dressing up etc.

Lao Tzu is comparing mighty army to dry wood. Dry wood is lifeless and so are the people waging war devoid of compassion for they have become killing machines.

After death man's body becomes rigid like a log of wood. This 'log of wood' will burn together in the funeral pyre alongwith other logs of wood. Lao Tzu compares rigidity in thinking to dry and dead trees which will eventually be felled down.

Let us try to loosen ourselves a little. As tight dresses come in the way of our activity and affect our blood circulation, rigidity of ideology will hinder the all round development that every human is capable of.

77th Verse

INVISIBLE GOODNESS

Perhaps the Way of Heaven may be likened to the stretching of a composite bow!
The upper part is depressed, while the lower is raised.
If the bow- string is too long, it is cut short:
if too short, it is added to.

The Way of Heaven diminishes the more-than-enough to supply the less-than-enough.
The way of man is different:
it takes from the less- than-enough to swell the more-than-enough.
Who except a man of the Tao can put his superabundant riches to the service of the world?

Therefore, the Sage does his work without setting any store by it,
accomplishes his task without dwelling upon it.
He does not want his merits to be seen.

Lao Tzu lived many centuries ago and as such his reference to weapons of war were axes, swords, bows and arrows etc. The weapons of mass destruction that we experience now were absent in those days.

The bow and arrow is another beautiful way to explain the co-existence of strength and suppleness supporting each other for the purpose for which they were made. The curved part of bow was made either from wood or some metal... the strong part of it. The ends were connected by string ...the supple part of it. The supple cannot afford to be sagging ...nor can it be made too tight that it snaps while tying it. The tension in the string has to be precise.

So much care goes into making bows and arrows. How much care is showered on us by Almighty while creating us! Learning to respect our abundance and putting it to common good will be another step towards Tao or God. We know that the water finds its own level. Water is just another creation of the Almighty. Even when water knows how to find balance, should we humans who are almost 75% water, not learn to balance?

78th Verse

POWER OF THE WEAKLING

Nothing in the world is softer and weaker than water;
But, for attacking the hard and strong, there is nothing like it!
For nothing can take its place.
That the weak overcomes the strong and the soft overcomes the hard,
This is something known by all, but practiced by none.

Therefore the Sage says:
To receive the dirt of a country is to be lord of its soil-shrines.
To bear the calamities of a country is to be price of the world.
Indeed, Truth sounds like its opposite!

We have learnt in school about power of nature in changing the topography of a place. We have also learnt about denudation, deposition and transportation and also soil erosion. Water plays a major role in the said phenomena. Along river beds, we can find smooth stones telling us the invisible power of water over it. The softness of water can chisel the hard stones. The message we can learn is 'never under estimate anything'.

We know that water cannons are used to disperse mob that go on a rampage.

Naturopathy also uses water as a part of their therapy.

Most of the rulers blame others for any misfortune of their land. If any good things happen, they want to take credit for it. 'Head I win and tail you lose' seem to be their attitude. Real virtue is to accept both profit and loss, good and bad with equal grace and stability of mind.

When Lao Tzu says "Dirt of the Country", maybe he is referring to the downtrodden people who are not respected by others. When you work for them, uplift them, you are constructing shrines. Every person that you thus uplift, you go on constructing shrine after shrine. Thus the whole world becomes one big shrine.

79th Verse

A SCAR CAN BE SCARY

When a great wound is healed,
there will still remain a scar.
Can this be a desirable state of affairs?
Therefore, the Sage holding the left-hand tally,
Performs his part of the covenant,
But lays no claims upon others.

The virtuous attends to his duties;
The virtue less knows only to levy duties upon the
people.
The Way of Heaven has no private affections,
But always accords with the good.

A physical wound is healed in course of time. But, it leaves behind a scar. Even if there is no scar, when we look at that particular place of injury, memory will revive and re-live the past. Even the now-invisible wound has the power to over-power us.

When I visited some place of worship in India, I felt such deep pain to see the ruins left behind by ruthless invaders. Such scars can never be healed.

Similarly, wars leave behind scars that are seldom healed. There is physical wound for the person involved in wars and emotional wound for his family members which are like festering wounds or ulcers.

What we now experience is war of words. Religious fanatics use their tongues as weapons. Inciting innocent and ignorant people about some so called ideology has created havoc in the world. Lao Tzu is referring to such wounds. It is the attitude, the behavior and the words spat out in anger and hatred which can never be healed.

The virtuous attends to his duties;
The virtue less knows only to levy duties upon the people.
The Way of Heaven has no private affections,
But always accords with the good.

What, according to Lao Tzu, is the difference between a man of virtue and a man lacking in virtue?

He says that a man of virtue performs all actions without expecting anything in return. He is aware of his duty towards his family and friends and also to the country he belongs to. As there is no expectation, there is no disappointment either. A man lacking in virtue will be seeking something in return for whatever he does. Expectations lead to disappointment. There can be disappointment if the person whom we oblige does not acknowledge our favour done to him. Many times, we get hurt because of such attitude of ingratitude.

Expectations are the invisible chains that bind us. Non-expectation is freedom! That is true happiness and to give a spiritual flavor, the ultimate *mukthi* or *nirvana* or enlightenment!

There have been kings and emperors who used to levy heavy taxes on their people, having no consideration about their financial capacity. A person who was not able to pay the taxes was severely punished. It was but natural that people revolted against them.Lao Tzu says that Heaven (or God) will always be with virtuous people.

80th Verse

SELF CONTAINED COMMUNITY

Ah, for a small country with a small population!
Though there are highly efficient mechanical contrivances,
the people have no use for them.
Let them mind death and refrain from migrating to distant places.
Boats and carriages, weapons and armour there may still be,
but there are no occasions for using or displaying them.
let the people revert to communication by knotting chords.
See to it that they are contented with their food,
pleased with their clothing, satisfied with their houses,
and inured to their simple ways of living.
Though there may be another country in the neighborhood so close that

they are within sight of each other and the crowing of cocks
and barking of dogs in one place can be heard in the other,
yet there is no traffic between them,
and throughout their lives the two peoples have nothing to do with each other.

Migration of villagers to towns has affected agricultural sector. This is very true especially in India. Apart from agriculture, local customs, arts and crafts also suffer. Few hundred years ago, people seldom left their place of origin. Whatever was locally available, be it food-grains, tools available or transportation, were used. Nature has provided particular type of grain, fruits and other natural products to a particular type of geographical condition which is better suited to people living there.

Mahatma Gandhi laid emphasis on developing each village as a separate unit of development so that migration to towns is minimal. He said: "Agriculture is the back bone of India". Just like our whole body is supported by our back bone, agriculture is the foundation of a country's economy. When you take care of your back bone, many of the physical ailments will be cured. India being a country of farmers, great importance must be given to them.

Lao Tzu describes a self-contained habitat. According to him, if each village becomes self-contained, many of the problems created by migration can be avoided. There will be peace in such places. Peace will result in good health of its people and they can lead a good life. One who lives in peace will also leave (die) in peace. This is an ideal way of living.

What we see now is family in fragments. The younger generation is far away from their parents. If our family members stay away from us for a long time, can we be happy, especially towards old age or final exit from this world? We have to ask ourselves.

Lao Tzu is suggesting a contented life where people enjoy simple food, simple clothing and simple living. After all, how much do we need? However tasty a food item may be, we cannot go on eating continuously!! Even if we posses hundreds of clothing, we cannot wear all of them one over the other.

Depending on the climatic conditions of the place we live, we can adjust our lifestyle as far as clothing is concerned. Even if we own a 20 bedroom apartment, all the 19 of them are somebody else's....as I need and can use only one room at a time.

Even if I own 1000 dresses, I can wear only one at a time. Such display of wealth is another invisible sickness ...the first sickness is greed. Who is the mother of greed?

Discontentment..Why such discontentment?...Because we have moved far away from Tao...

The master says that:

Though there may be another country in the neighborhood so close that
they are within sight of each other and the crowing of cocks
and barking of dogs in one place can be heard in the other,
yet there is no traffic between them,

and throughout their lives the two peoples have nothing to do with each other.

While describing about self-contained places of dwelling, he also says that a dog barking or a crow cawing can be heard by the other villages. That means though they are independent, they are not very far away from each other. While living in proximity of each other, and yet enjoying our unique life style is what he is emphasizing upon. An Utopian Dream? No, a reality which you can join in.

81th Verse

LIFE OF A KARMA YOGI

Sincere words are not sweet,
Sweet words are not sincere.
Good men are not argumentative,
the argumentative are not good.
The wise are not erudite,
the erudite are not wise.

The Sage does not take to hoarding.
The more he lives for others, the fuller is his life.
The more he gives, the more he abounds.

The Way of Heaven is to benefit, not to harm.
The Way of the Sage is to do his duty,
not to strive with anyone.

A Sanskrit verse says; *sulabaha purusha rajan satatam priyavadinaha..apriyascha patyascha vakta shrota cha durlabaha*. It means that it is easy to find people who talk sweetly; But when it comes to things that are not pleasant to hear but are beneficial, it is difficult to find a speaker as well as a listener. Great orators need not necessarily be persons of great wisdom; nor a man in silence be regarded as less intelligent.

What is oratory? It is nothing but accumulated information presented in a beautiful way. A person with good memory, some command over a language and knowing how to present his ideas to create an impact on the listener is considered as a good orator.

Is memory wisdom? Can presentation skill be termed as wisdom? Can mastery of a language be termed as wisdom?

As we saw in one of the previous chapters, Lord Buddha many times went in silence.

After that inner silence, the words that came out were full of wisdom. That wisdom sustains the millions of his followers. Lao Tzu says; the argumentative are not good.

Many times, people argue endlessly to prove their point. Such people have command over their language. It is another form of ego, which always wants to prove itself.

A wise man has said that it is better to lose an argument that to lose a friend.

An egoistic person is seldom liked by people around him. An argumentative person is avoided by many as they know in their wisdom, the futility of opening any conversation with such people.

Having come to the battle field to wage war against the Kauravas, Arjuna is reluctant to take up arms. He is humbly requesting Krishna to please accept him as His disciple and guide him as to what he (Arjuna) is supposed to do. Till that question was asked, Krishna did not advise him about what he was supposed to do. Krishna does not advise until asked for! Such humility!

The word 'hoarding' is used not just the accumulated wealth or property. On a deeper level, it also means showing off of one's knowledge as some people like to display their accumulated wealth. A man of Tao will always do his best for others. While doing his duty he has no desire for a 'return gift'.

'Return gift' is expecting something ...even if we expect a word of appreciation or a word of thanks, we are put into this bracket of 'return gift'. If the desire for gift is unfulfilled, we have to 'return' to collect the same. This is the root cause of re-birth.

The ever-fresh wisdom of Lao Tzu and divine message of Lord Krishna when understood in the right perspective and acted upon with diligence will create a new world. Thus we come to a holy beginning.

———◆❖◆———

About the Author

Can a house-holder live a life dedicated to God? Is it possible to follow karma yog as propogated by Lord Krishna to Arjuna? Questions like these haunted Pramila Iyer, the author. She found her answers being with her gurus and thus became a ardent student of philosophy. She experienced great freedom and inexplicable joy. She started conducting classes on Karma Yog and Bhaja Govindam. As a person with varied interest, her classes were always inter-active The participants enthusiastically enacted the scenes in her sessions. Her faith in greatness of every individual brought out the otherwise shy and hesitant participants to come forward and be a part of the extempore skits and dramas. Unparalleled Parallels is her fifth book. She has written books on Vasanta Sai and Satya Sai Baba. Her book Pranayam Khelkhelmein is a fresh approach to doing pranayam. Rainbows are Real is a collection of her poems that reflect her feeling towards cruelty to animals and other social issues typical of Indian back-ground. She also writes poems in Hindi and Tamil, her mother tongue. Her articles and short stories are in the process of coming out in the form of a book. She is also involved with under-privileged children's education and has been giving free tuitions since last 35 years. "A hungry stomach knows no God" involves her in doing her bit to offer food to humans and animals.